D0571879

A Sabbath Life

A Sabbath Life

A Woman's Search for
Wholeness

KATHLEEN HIRSCH

North Point Press
A division of Farrar, Straus and Giroux

Library of Congress Cataloging-in-Publication Data
Hirsch, Kathleen.
   A Sabbath life : one woman's search for wholeness / Kathleen Hirsch —
1st ed.
      p.   cm.
   ISBN 0-86547-598-9 (hardcover : alk. paper)
   1. Life.   2. Hirsch, Kathleen.   3. Feminists—Biography.   I. Title.
BD435 .H57 2001
818'.5409—dc21
[B]
                                                        2001018685

Designed by Cassandra J. Pappas

"Heart-bird" used by permission of the estate of Linda J. Corrente.

To Elisabeth Dyssegaard

There is no linear evolution; there is only a circumambulation of the self. Uniform development exists, at most, only at the beginning; later, everything points towards the center.

— CARL JUNG

I don't believe in aging. I believe in forever altering one's aspect to the sun.

— VIRGINIA WOOLF

Contents

ONE

Turning Forty

A DREAM

I am sitting in a room high above a city of hills. The light is turquoise and white, brilliant turquoise from the sea, brilliant white from the sun glancing off stucco compounds that form a continuous epic of habitation as they descend to the place where they began centuries ago, by the boats where boys still dive for the day's food.

I am waiting. I am waiting without impatience or urgency. I look out on the hills in the distance and at the azure sea below through the open arches that form three walls of my room. Above my head is the same unimpeded openness, the endless turquoise sky.

This room is my private chamber, and I dwell in it by virtue of a lifetime's devotion to the sacred mysteries. My collection of sea-shells sits alongside my pens and paper and my wisdom texts. A carved chest at the foot of my bed holds my needlework. My needs are thus more or less completely satisfied.

The simplicity and sensuality of the room mark it as a distinctly womanly place. Indeed, the atmosphere of the dream, with its scent of incense and salt water, my white and azure robe, the lapis and opals that I wear in my ears, all seem to suggest that in this room I sustain the deep truths of the feminine.

One detail in particular seems to affirm this. It is the bed. The bed is the most beautiful object in the room. It is draped with a

3

coverlet into which has been stitched a kind of compendium. In vivid threads and entwining vines, creatures of the sea and air and land depict the tale of Eden.

It is more than an ornament, this spread. It suggests itself as a text, a statement about the relation of the woman to the rest of creation, which one might learn to read, if given the time and the proper keys. As indeed I, the dreamer, must learn if I am ever to become the dreamed.

The "I" of the dream is a different matter altogether. Not only is she at ease among her books and the objects and creatures that are her companions. It was she who created them, she who stitched them. She is at once familiar and Delphic, at home with the earth-bound lessons of Eden, with the timeless mysteries of Greece, Byzantium, and Jerusalem. She might be in Turkey or in India, in the East or the West. In my dream, they are one and the same. She transcends time and geography.

As I said, she is waiting. She is waiting for the arrival of a lover, or to stitch, or to read a page from the book of wisdom. All of these, the detachment and engagement, the passion and the poem, the flesh and the page, are one and the same.

AT THE START of this story I am standing in a field of something that I can't name, taking in the heady scent of it. I do not have the names for any of the multitude of things that grow or fly or flower in front of me. Not the fruit trees, not the flowers, not the birds.

For twenty years I have occupied the same room of life that I have called my career. I have worked twelve to fifteen hours a day, on weekends as well. What I have achieved—my relevance, my currency, my visibility—has constituted my sense of who I am.

I am childless. My relations with my family and friends are minimal, defended, graciously superficial. My marriage is settled. My home with its collection of handmade pots and art books, spare. I attend symphony, see the season's major art exhibits, and spend long country weekends with friends who do the same.

I do not know the names of the wisdom books that I would gather around me because, though once a student of poetry, philosophy, and art, I have become a purveyor of facts. I would need a lover of the stature of my dream to stir in me the deep ecstasy that flitted briefly through midnight. I am no longer sure of the names of my feelings, or the currents of my desires.

As I stand and gaze at all of which I am so appallingly ignorant in the natural world, in the geography of my dream life, in the indistinct reach of my desires, tears come to my eyes and I hear the words of my beloved Proust:

"We must rediscover that reality from which we become separated as the formal knowledge we substitute for it grows in thickness and imperviousness—that reality which there is grave danger we may die without having known, and which is simply our life."

It has not yet occurred to me that there might be another woman, or several, inside of me. I wouldn't know what to do with such information. I have been trained to believe in the "achieving self" as the ultimate goal and justification of life.

A graduate of a Seven Sisters college, with an advanced degree from an Ivy League university, I believe that women ought to assert themselves in a manner similar to that which for generations had been sanctioned by and for men.

Specifically, I accept that this self-expression is to be accomplished according to the same norms of success, the same terms of performance, the same operative structures, as men's.

———

AT TIMES, it has been exhilarating.

It has greatly simplified the substrate of warring motives and unwanted ambivalences that has occasionally appeared.

Over the years it has grown easier and easier to accept the lost parts of the Self as the inevitable cost of maturation and success . . .

＊

THE WOMAN of my dream caught up with me. In a rare moment of vulnerability she of the lost wisdom, buried for years in the detritus of ambition and distraction, confronted me with my own inner fragmentation. She demanded to know why it was necessary to surrender parts of myself in order to be successful.

I began to wonder if achievement could take a form uniquely my own *as a woman*, and whether my mature vision of what matters in life, and the means of best going about what matters, might quite naturally and inevitably part company with men's; indeed whether it might not contribute something of unique and irreplaceable value to the culture in which I live.

This is the story of a journey of awakening. My intention is to share my efforts to achieve in my middle years a wholeness that I did not know (and didn't care to find) as a younger woman. Simply by listening to my inner soundings, and to the many inspiring women whom I have met over the past few years, I have learned what it means to genuinely honor the Self. Today I live a life not as the culture would have me live it, but as I understand its underlying purposes from within.

Success is a manifold and changing thing. When women embrace their own ways of seeing and attempting to influence the realities around them, their norms of what is sacred, and their seasons, they create lives that are varied, abundant, fruitful, and, at day's end, rich in wisdom and peace. Sabbath lives. In honoring what makes us women, we transform the world around us.

Whether absorbed in a career as I have been, or at home with children, or attempting some more individual balance between achievement, relationship, and service, every woman has the deep reserves within her to create such a life. To begin, she needs only to listen.

THE LOST ELEMENTS

$\mathcal{B}eauty$

1

MY FRIEND LINDA and her husband have loaned us their country house for two weeks in August while they hike in Montana. The drive from Boston takes about two and a half hours. We wend our way through beautiful rolling hills thick with summer's green into a valley speckled with steepled towns, horse farms, and swaying sunflowers. All summer long, I have been adrift. A book project three long and hard years in progress is mired in a tangle of insurmountable obstructions: uncooperative sources, key players hostile to my presence as a researcher.

But something else is at work too. I can't deny the inertia that has begun to sap my energy. I am constantly tired. Undermotivated. I've begun to prefer the solitude of my deck to the company of friends. And I can't put my finger on the cause of these changes in me.

We arrive midmorning. I no sooner unpack than I fall into bed and sleep for two hours.

I am awakened by the toot of an antique pickup that has pulled up to the front door. It is the groundskeeper, with a gift of early apples picked somewhere else on the property. Tart-smelling and sharp, small and still partially green, they are what a good apple ought to be, so much so that I want to arrange them for display in one of the wooden bowls.

"No," he says, following me into the kitchen. "You need to eat them now. Their skins are soft. If you don't, they'll rot."

Obligingly, I take one outdoors and watch the plume of dust that rises from his rattling departure down the hill. The chickadees are fighting at the feeders. Banks of phlox are shaking morning dew off the bachelor buttons.

I look at the apple. Under normal circumstances, I would save it for later and make it lunch. In the past I've considered a retreat like the one I am just beginning "stolen" time. Cheater's time. But as I stand in the dappled shade of an old tree, for the first time in many months I begin to remember what peace feels like. It almost seems that life is offering me something that I haven't even known I've needed. I bite into the apple.

IT IS GOOD to be in Linda's space. I spend the mornings on a bench overlooking a paddock where a pair of horses graze, glossy under cloud-scudding skies. In the upper meadow beyond them, I can occasionally make out hawks and wild turkey, chipmunks and a goose cavorting between the brush and the tall oaks.

In the afternoons, I go back indoors, curl up on the sofa, and read. Or I try to. As the days go by, I find myself increasingly diverted by the objects Linda has chosen to display on sills and tabletops, on the mantel and along the margins of crowded book-shelves. Birds' eggs retrieved from the forest floor, feathers as broad as my palm. Abandoned nests and small fish fossils and bones blanched white from the sun that captures their blazes like pieces of polished marble.

Quietly, I observe them. Do they seem more wonderful because they are cameos, plucked from the untidy wilds? Or is it just that their perfectly realized natures stand in such sharp contrast to the paltriness of my own harried and fragmentary efforts at a similar sort of completeness? I begin to feel them working on me in subtle ways. In the absolute stillness of these August afternoons, they seem to proffer an invitation. Dispense with your preoccupations, they say, and join us in a shared "hereness," in this never to be repeated Now.

I realize all of a sudden that I have always felt this way in Linda's habitats, whether in one of her several Manhattan addresses or in the many rooms she lived in throughout college and graduate school. And as the days pass, I find my thoughts more and more inclining toward the artifacts' silent urgings, away from my own malaise and toward Linda, to the points of fierce connection and contrast that have marked our twenty-year friendship as women, as writers, as feminists. Oddly, this doesn't feel like an evasion of the near-paralysis from which I am in flight, but a way of moving into it from what is perhaps a deeper, more reliable vantage.

✳

I MET LINDA the autumn of my junior year in college when I chanced into the room she shared with the cartoonist for the college newspaper, who was a friend of mine. Mount Holyoke in the mid-'70s was a hothouse of feminist sympathies. The student paper, classes, dinner conversations, all were seedbeds for a discussion that took many forms and expressed itself in many ways but that, even when the last lights went out in libraries and dorms, seemed to linger in the unfinished tendrils of passionate talk that filled the night air.

When Gloria Steinem spoke about women and power, we

listened. When Susan Brownmiller chronicled women's historic abuse, we cheered her on. By the light of these new and forceful voices, we were rewriting our lives.

No one was immune to the energies that feminism released in us. We were not doctrinaire: There were as many ways to be a feminist in those days as there were women to interpret its message for themselves. But interpret we expected one another to do. Some of us were reordering the curricula. Others were setting up independent feminist houses, trying out ways of organizing life that they hoped to carry into the world beyond the campus gates. We were trying out identities—as artists, doctors, physicists, liberated from the barriers that had stymied so many of our mothers.

I found Linda sitting on the floor of her room smoking a cigarette and doing something intricate with a stylus and a piece of coated metal. The air held a musk of incense, as if just that morning her lover had come and gone. She had exquisite hands, and as we exchanged introductions, I watched them, fascinated.

She was preparing a plate for etching. Around her lay several beautiful, hand-stitched chapbooks. On her desk were several more, lying open beneath the eye of a magnificent horn that had been carved into the head of a crane. Scattered throughout the room were bunches of dried grasses and pods that she had gathered from the fields that extended out from the campus before climbing into the foothills of the Holyoke range.

She was elegant and large of presence, with dazzling sea-blue eyes and a quick, deep laugh.

We began talking about our lives. Linda was a poet. She had the sharp, omnivorous mind of a classicist. I was writing political commentary for the campus newspaper and privately, in the dead of night, my own poems and short fiction. We were both fiercely unorthodox in our academic habits, routinely flouting assignments to pursue our own intellectual interests. She was reading Blake at the time. I, the French existentialists and the poetics of despair. She had a weakness for sensual beauty. I, for elegant systems. It was immediately obvious that there would be no end to what we had to say to one another.

We became inseparable. During the long afternoons of that fall, we often worked together in silence. When we weren't writing or reading, breaking to share a sentence or the phrase of some poem with the other, we were in the art studio. Linda worked in mass, casting bronze sculptures and printing large works on paper. I experimented with drawing and with various calligraphic traditions.

Many evenings of that magical fall, just before dinner, we would close our books, don jackets, and climb into her car. Without maps, and with little more than a vague destination in mind, we'd drive out into the farmland that ran along the Connecticut River between South Hadley and Northampton. Often, we were the only vehicle in sight at that hour, motoring along the dirt roads in search of a path to hike, a summit to climb, a stretch of natural beauty to cleanse and correct us after days spent lodged in the mind—preferably one that would reward us with a water view as we sat and watched the sun set together.

I have kept the slides that I made of our favorite spot. It was a hill overlooking the buried towns of the vast Quabbin Reservoir in western Massachusetts. In one photograph, the sun spins bronze over the blue clay of the hills. A heron floats below us, coursing close to the islands of a dark archipelago. It is serene, hungry, and wild—a creature so stately and intent it seems a being out of time. Linda and I went there many times after this, to watch the same scene and to search for the same heron. It came to be ours, as we came to be safe havens for each other, wild and serene in our own ways, silently grateful to be able to be all of this with another.

And so the months went by. I felt Linda's presence making me a more willing participant in the life of beauty than I—so preoccupied by my desire to change the world—had been for a long time.

*

MY HUSBAND RETURNS from his hike and runs the tap in the kitchen, and I am rousted back to the present. After many years of marriage, he, a newspaper editor, has cultivated a good barometer of my need for large chunks of silence. Since we've arrived he has given me just what I need. I hear the screen door slam and his tread across the pine bed to the hammock.

In a moment, I will follow him. But just now I am struck by how utterly I've let beauty slip away. The herons are gone from my life. What happened to the coherence and integrity that as a younger woman I managed to achieve by allowing my nature to express its needs and desires freely? I no longer give myself the time to drink deeply of contemplated beauty, no longer allow it to work on me, to replenish my soul. And I haven't, I realize, for many years.

*

WHEN THE SNOW BEGAN to thaw the following spring, Linda took me to visit her family home and the places that had yielded their images to her first poems.

As we traveled across Massachusetts on a soft spring evening, dipped into Rhode Island, and continued to its southern regions, I encountered an unknown geography. Around us to the east and west lay the ocean. I couldn't see it, but it seemed to saturate everything, the smell of the air, the quality of the dying light. Within its powerful arms stretched a landscape salt-chewed and wind-burned, of rusted shacks and middens in the middle of nowhere, of bent orchards and oaks, of sun-scalded lighthouses and ribbons of crushed shells digging their hieroglyphs into sand. Even the hills in proportion to the low trees, the ancient stone walls, seemed to couch themselves in a deft parenthesis. The accommodation of form to ocean furl, of fresh to salt, of wound to renewal, was everywhere in a breathtaking, gentle grace. It struck my eye as perfect in scale, as classical as Linda's mind.

In the morning, we stepped out through the sliding glass doors of her living room to the grassy slope that dipped down to a large pond. Geese and gulls came to its surface and left, familiar as the heron we'd left behind. Without a word, Linda turned and indicated that I should follow her. She pursued an imperceptible path along the banks of the pond for several minutes, then cut into the woods that stood not far from the house. We walked another two hundred yards in, then came to a stop, and I found myself standing before a small shingled cabin.

"My father built this for me when I was sixteen, so that I could come here and write," she said.

We went in. It was wonderful: unfinished planks and beams, a window overlooking the water, a wicker chair, a lamp, and a place for a few books.

Of course, we'd both read Virginia Woolf's *A Room of One's Own*. It was one of our sacred texts. But Linda was the first person I'd met for whom a space apart for creative solitude had been no mere fantasy.

In the afternoon, we went to the shore. There is nothing tame or parenthetical about the Rhode Island coast, and this is its glory. It is chalk and stone ruins, miles of pampas grass and wild, beautiful tides. It is cove upon cove of uncompromising natural force.

We sat at a place called Galilee with the winds buffeting us, the surf crashing, and I felt Linda filling herself up with its healing salt, the pieces of her extraordinary struggles with the world and its beauty falling once again into place.

A champion swimmer and honors student, she'd gone to England the summer she was sixteen to study poetry at Oxford. Midway through, however, she found herself struggling with a miasma of confusion and exhaustion. Sent back home, she was diagnosed with a rare thyroid disorder, which was only provisionally treatable. She would have to be monitored and medicated for the rest of her life. She would never know when a sudden wave of mental fog might incapacitate her, when a hormonal storm would throw off her medication, or how long a certain treatment would be effective before the cycle of experimentation would have to begin again.

That summer, she spent hours staring at the tides and walking the beach, searching for meaning in the face of her sudden, inescapable limitations and uncertainties. The ocean that had once been a place of free and easy joy acquired a far more complex imagery, the first of many that her landscape offered the spirit that grieved in her.

If the ocean absorbed her fear and rage, the interior farmlands with their vineyards, the small hilltop monastery where she was a communicant, offered her evidence of a mitigating human culture in the face of nature's random destructive force. It gave her back a sense of possibility and hope. If the ocean was untamable, the fields of apples and rye were witnesses of life-giving form. She ferried these images, the stones and feathers, the mythic shapes and the silence of the natural world back to her small cabin. There, with her senses fired, she gathered and wove and arranged them into her own small and perfect shapes of hope.

Again and again in the course of that weekend, I was able to see how the weft of her days passed between cabin, field, shore, and back again had saturated her sensibility and woven in her a faith embedded not just in words, but in the gift of nature. Again and again, I saw how our meeting had been for me one of those gifts, from a not wholly governable source.

AT THE SAME TIME that Linda was forging her way through despair to the creative within her, several hundred miles away I was traveling each day to a private girls' convent school. There I was learning that beauty was a house of many stories. I read Yeats and Wallace Stevens for hours on end. With a fairly polished command of French, I read Racine and Montaigne, Hugo and Beckett. I dreamed of living in Paris, free of domestic responsibility, writing and flouting the conventions of my bourgeois childhood.

This was a useful fantasy. At sixteen, I still managed to "pass" in my convivial middle-class world of professional fathers and stay-at-home moms. Come Friday night, I went with my friends to the dances at the nearby boys' schools. Come spring, I took a role in their musicals and plays. On weekends, I modeled clothing for downtown clothing stores.

But I knew that not all forms of beauty were equal. Indeed, it was becoming increasingly clear to me that beauty's multiple forms could be divided. There were those that elicited temporary triumphs and those that touched my deepest reaches, that stirred the silence in me to some rare and precious song. The first order of beauty was profligate, fleeting, diffusive. The other, enduring. As I surveyed the well-meaning conventions that would lead me to a life among the first forms, I felt a powerful instinct to choose—to turn away—if I was to survive as a self.

Between the life of the intellect and the life of the senses, between Chekhov and Cole Porter, between a life of creativity and a life of charity balls, stood the one obvious bargaining chip: my own body.

Starvation for me was not a quest for physical beauty, but rather a way to tunnel through the physical to the spiritual.

THE WILL IS so exacting. So unforgiving. I longed to attach myself to something inviolate, something that would never be corrupted by the demands that life seemed to make upon its women. This was not a political act, but a spiritual one.

I stopped going to dances. The romantic interests of my friends ceased to interest me. I preferred reading to just about anything else, because in reading, I was able to escape into the abiding questions—and, I was ever hopeful, ⁺ˡ ir answers. My mind was constantly at work, high on its binge .eason, of judgment, of honing itself like a jeweler's tool to find the perfect edge, the flawless facet in the stone. As my plaid school skirt became more gaping around the waist, as my bracelets slipped from my arms, I became very good at discerning the less-than, the mediocre, the ugly.

But somehow in the process, what was true and good and beautiful seemed daily to be reduced by another fraction as well. I didn't see that in the attempt to protect something of value, I was making it invisible—almost to the point of vanishing. By some inexplicable kind of reciprocal negation—I was by now twenty-five pounds underweight—I had to entertain the possibility that I would find at the end of my quest not truth, but only infinite emptiness.

Paris once had been the secret dream. Now, though I had almost stopped searching for what I had ceased to find, I still maintained a detached, cold curiosity about the capital city of a lost self. In the middle of that nightmarish winter, much against their better judgment, my parents allowed me to accompany a group of classmates there for two weeks.

Paris that February was frigid. In seven days, I ate part of an egg, a bite of a meringue, a half cup of black tea. Because I was still starving myself to death and now knew it, I was always cold.

On a small street just off the rue de Rivoli twenty-six years ago, there stood a public scale. One morning into the second week, very early, I went alone and dropped my centimes in. I weighed eighty-eight pounds and I knew that the blue wool coat that I wore to ward off the chill probably accounted for five of them. It would be easy now, I knew, and not for very long.

I wandered on. The city was just waking up, misty and gray. Bare trees gathered their doves, then dropped them on the morning's wet stones like so many fallen leaves. I passed no one for several sur-real blocks. I was aware of my heart, laboring.

The stores were just opening. At the corner, I found myself in front of Rosenthal's. Its broad glass entrance was already open. To escape the bone-numbing cold, I went inside. The warmth and the quiet of the showroom at that early hour were comforting.

Mercifully, the clerks left me alone, for I had gone into a sort of trance. I moved very slowly from case to case, ghosting from object to object. Gold-leafed dinnerware, goblets, and blown-glass fig-urines were arrayed for a banquet that would never take place. Around them were apples and grapevines, hand-painted cornu-copias burgeoning with a harvest of blown glass.

Many of the pieces were transparent, crystal squirrels and acorns, creatures of sky, field, and forest. They were unreal on gray velvet in the glass cases before me, and I was taking them in more at the level of dream than of consciousness. At some point, I stopped, unable to move away. Some ultimate part of me, some sanity, that felt at the moment a bit like love, rose and bent over me where I hovered at the glass.

Perhaps the obvious imminence of my mortality had finally bro-ken through. Perhaps the cumulative force of Paris's manifold beauties had coalesced in that moment of crisis. Perhaps the same event would have occurred had I stumbled on an empty bottle or an open bookstall. I'll never know.

What I do know is that as an anonymous and nearly transparent young woman adrift in a European capital, I suddenly felt a life-saving kinship with these objects. They touched me more deeply than words. They were transparent, integral, like crystal poems. They were all that I wanted to be.

In them, I saw that matter could be transformed into beauty, but remain matter, not principle. Beauty, the soul's medium, could not simply be intellectualized. It had to be embodied, or it would die. Cut off from this need for a space in the world, it wasn't beauty that died, it was the soul.

Out of the spinning feast of color beneath me, I fixed on a cup that symbolized this insight the way a seashell holds the residue of a wave. Out of all the gifts that Paris had to offer, out of all that I could have chosen as a memento of its somber and storied beauties, I foraged in the pocket of my coat for my carefully hoarded savings and spilled them on the counter. When I left the shop, I was carrying that cup, smaller than my hand, an object meant to contain what for a long and painful season I had been unwilling to consume.

I hadn't realized how hungry I was. I was seventeen.

LINDA BECAME the force of reconnection in my life. In her presence, I was able to take in the beauty of the waves, the stones that we gathered and tossed as we talked, the warmth of the sand.

I had tried to separate what, in a thing of beauty, can't be separated, the mortal shape from the eternal truth. In so doing, I'd lost touch with the nature of the beautiful, its concreteness, and embodiment, and particularity. Beauty simply *was*. It didn't need to be justified. It didn't require a philosophical analog to truth. It contained within it truths that couldn't be pried from their métier and forced to lie, thin and cold, beneath the glass of analytical inquiry without losing their essential life.

We stayed at the beach that weekend eating crab cakes and drinking Cokes every day until dusk. We talked about Virginia Woolf, and about her artist sister, Vanessa.

What had made their work possible, we wondered, so original? Their lives so passionate, vivid, and full?

Space and time, we decided.

But I knew that there was something else as well. All their lives, Virginia and Vanessa complemented one another, protected one another, and in their art inspired one another. Though Linda and I in no way ever explicitly compared ourselves to Virginia Woolf and Vanessa Bell—would, in fact, have found it arrogant and a bit silly to do so—in many ways our relationship *had* come to resemble theirs.

Of the two of us, I was the more intense, cerebral, more psychological. I was far more likely to bury myself in the library until I was so exhausted that I had to check myself into the infirmary for several days. Linda was uniquely able to pull me out of my inner world. She would drive me to the beach, leave a cluster of wild daisies at my door, lure me to a seedy backwoods club to drink cheap Chablis and listen to jazz.

Linda was my complement: the colorist, the sensualist, the gardener, bird lover, and an alchemist in the kitchen. What seemed possible for us in our lives was much the same as had seemed possible in Virginia's and Vanessa's. And much of the *sense* of these possibilities arose from, and abided in, the intensity of our bond. Without our ambles together, without the fertile intermingling of the many ways of being a woman that I experienced when I was with her, I would have become brittle, narrow, driven.

In time, Linda became editor of the campus literary magazine, I, the executive editor of the newspaper. We were at peace with our differences.

The following fall, our senior year, we had a conversation that I will never forget. We were picking tomatoes in the garden of a house she'd rented near campus, when suddenly Linda began playing at imagining our respective futures. Again, the comparison with Virginia Woolf and Vanessa Bell came up.

I was to be the writer, far more likely to live with a lover, we decided, than to settle into any more domestic arrangement. Linda knew just what she wanted.

"I want to be Vanessa," she remarked.

She was going to marry a painter and have five children. She would write poetry in the mornings and bake bread with them each afternoon on an open brick hearth. She would make everything possible in the house—dishes, furniture, the art that hung on the walls.

"Doesn't that sound *perfect?*" she demanded to know in that flashing way of hers. "I would be so happy!"

When she said this, it seemed so *right.* All at once, I could see her as the great earth mother, the Vanessa, for both of us, tolerantly filling up my spirit with her boundlessly generous one whenever I visited over the years, offering my pearls, my thoughts and ideas, for her bread and roses, her clay and earth. And in old age, when husband and lover were long gone, both of us assumed, we would come together again, picking up the intimacy that a lifetime of maturity had only deepened.

When Linda moved to New York and Columbia's writing program, I stayed behind and took a newspaper job, intending to eventually go to graduate school myself.

THERE ARE many ways to bury the Self. Success is one of them. I worked for a daily paper for two years, then spent another two years in graduate school writing fiction, then took a job at a countercultural weekly newspaper in Boston, combining, so I convinced myself, these divergent experiences in writing features on city life and the women of its marginal subcultures.

I enjoyed the work. I liked my bohemian colleagues and the funky offices where arts reviewers and left-wing political hangers-on were constantly dropping in, and where columnists routinely fortified themselves with a swig of something from the lower drawer.

I was intellectually challenged and satisfied that in terms of its objective merits as useful, responsible, and successful, my work held up.

Linda *did* marry her painter. Their small flat in the Village was a continual disarray of drop cloths and poem fragments, shabby antiques and good, strong coffee. The sound of Italian opera floated four stories above West Eleventh Street at all hours of the night and day. I visited as often as I could.

But after a few years, Linda and R. went their separate ways. Linda took a day job with a writer's organization, editing its newsletter. She had never done anything by half-measures, and she wasn't about to do so now. She determined to make the newsletter the most successful writer's magazine in the country. Even after she married again, it was the magazine that shaped her continuing sense of purpose. She loved supporting the work of other writers and did so tirelessly, in personal relationships, over the many dinners that she and her husband hosted in the city and the country, and through the magazine, long after she had put her own active poetry work aside.

When she wasn't editing, she was studying Italian, bird watching, and entertaining a nearly full-time stream of houseguests. I was one of them.

There was never enough time in those years. My visits became increasingly intermittent. I was always rushing, always had three things to do at the same time, and this was particularly true when I went to New York. I took the earliest train so that I could work on the way down without distraction. Once there, I took cabs to avoid delays as I rushed to interviews or my agent's office. Once or twice a year, I'd dash uptown and see her for an hour but rarely for deep conversation or lasting insights. At day's end, I'd catch a cup of bad coffee with my brother at a stand-up shop outside Penn Station while I waited for my train. Then I'd work all the way home.

I was fulfilling the agenda I'd set myself in the context of the feminism of my twenties. I was writing about women at risk, wounded women, and the programs that helped them to heal and lead better lives. About safe houses and the rebuilding of self-esteem, about the skills damaged women need to become self-sufficient. This seemed the most important contribution that I could make, as a woman and as a writer.

But in reality, the work had taken on a life of its own. I was so caught up in the causes I was writing about that I didn't have time for a life of my own. Whatever else I'd succeeded at, I'd created an existence that shielded me from the ironies that lay everywhere around me, if only I was able to see.

My first book was published to favorable reviews. I was invited on speaking tours, television talk shows, panels. In professional terms, I couldn't have hoped for more.

I accepted another book contract, cleaned out my old files, and went through the rituals of beginning new research. But I had a hard time focusing on the voluminous reports and interview notes that I began to collect. For reasons I couldn't understand, I found it hard to work in my office. I was constantly tired.

Like many a good professional woman before me, I responded to these "work-related" pressures by finding a good therapist.

I joined a health club. I was working out three times a week, as often as possible with supportive women friends.

I soon intensified my therapy sessions to twice a week.

It was in this state that I'd come to Connecticut.

✳

ON MY SEVENTH MORNING HERE, I wake at dawn with a pounding headache. It is Sunday, I vaguely realize, the day of rest. I get up and go downstairs to make coffee, passing the outlines, transcript drafts, and laboriously organized studies I've brought with me. I expect, as usual, that with my coffee I'll become instantly, compulsively verbal. I expect to do what I've done for so many years now, fill more pages with words that get me through another day in a life that has become increasingly unsupportable.

Instead, I sit down in the rocker by the fireplace.

Beyond the broad glass of the picture window, the finch feeders have been placed so that I am looking up into the thrilling choreography of birds in motion. The cocoons and periwinkles, the twig weavings of abandoned nests, the vertebral tracings of sea urchins, dried seed pods and blanched skulls, seem this morning to represent the deep sources of all that I have ever found beautiful, their memory and their forms.

Why, if I find all of this so beautiful—I get up and move slowly around the room, running my hand over a robin's egg, a nautilus shell—do I want to cry?

I take in the smell of old fires and cedar, of basil and pepper and candle wax, of earth and time.

What has Linda understood about the meaning of life that I have overlooked, dismissed, or simply forgotten along the way? How could we have set out from such similar places and arrived at such different destinations?

This question seems to draw me to the very brink of all that I know. Beyond I can see nothing. No answer. A nullity.

Then in the silence of the half-light, I hear a sound. Somewhere outdoors, but close enough for me to make out the creaking of a nest, baby chicks are being born.

As the Paul Simon song goes, "Sometimes even music cannot substitute for tears."

I've been hearing that line in my head for weeks. Finally, I sink into the rocker and weep. They are tears of exhaustion, frustration, and grief. The clay pot that has held my life is cracking. I know, without knowing exactly *what* I know, that the fissures are deeper than a book project gone sour. My life seems in shards, not a bulwark for my soul but a driven taskmaster of my will.

I've lost my way. I've been so secure in my pot, a well-developed perennial specimen. I've surveyed and sampled the environment around me, habituated to a way of being that *worked*.

But this is just the trouble. It is a formula I've been living, a code of care and watering instructions that I wrote for myself when I was twenty and have spent these many years perfecting. Now, it is clear, they are failing me. Or I, failing them.

I am literally starving, have been starving for years, for something profound, something elemental that I have not dared to discover.

*

I HAVE BEEN up the hill that rises behind the meadow once, years earlier, with Linda. It was the same time of year, the time of raspberries and lady apples, of ripe corn and tall grass that smells like hay with the sun burning down through patches in the pines. We brought bread and cheese that day, olives and a bottle of wine. We made a feast of it, as years earlier we'd made a feast of hills and farmland.

After a cup of coffee and a bowl of fresh raspberries, I start up empty-handed. As I climb through hemlocks and low-lying bushes, I think of the bobcat we heard several nights ago, shrieking like a woman under torture. Fear rises and I push it away.

I am not in the grip of reason, I am in the zone of faith. I am doing what I am doing because something in me, some remembered self, tells me that I must.

I remember the birch grove overlooking the lake at college where I anchored myself with a book many afternoons. I remember the farms along the Connecticut River and the craggy outcrops of Skinner Mountain where we used to hunt for sunsets.

Slowly, as I ascend, time falls away. And I feel myself being reclaimed by the silence of those moments. I become a being out of time.

I've gone halfway up when I am struck by a shaft of sun breaking through from above. Without understanding, I am flooded — simply, completely — with happiness.

I lie down in the grass and stretch out my arms. I let my fingers dig into the rich, dark earth. I cannot be more exposed, more vulnerable, if I were to try. And suddenly I realize that this is precisely what I need to be. I need to be vulnerable, to feel again the sensation of susceptible awe, the redemptive quality of beauty, the joy of simply being alive.

In a wash of memory, I see all of the moments in the past twenty years when I've veered toward beauty, only to push it away. Steeped in liberation politics, I sought a sort of grounding in handwork, projects that form several generations of baby gifts for friends. In a resolutely secular life, I possessed an irrational yearning to visit the quiet monastery an hour's drive from home. I wanted to write poems but never had the nerve, wanted to learn ancient languages but never made the time. On vacation, I spent my time in Romanesque churches and in the rear seats of vast cathedrals. I never spoke of any of these things to anyone. They seemed irrelevant, anti-intellectual, peculiar quirks that I appeased covertly or sublimated.

This hill, with its greens and early golds, its cardinals and black-berries, its distant scent of orchards, is paradise. It is beauty of a depth and complexity and interdependence that in my entire life-time I will never come close to exhausting with my share of under-standing or of wonder.

I want to write out of such a deep sense of the world, its underly-ing structures, not just its evanescent realities and issues. I want to work, as I once did, from my own felt connection to life and its depths, to use words drawn from the silence around and within me. I want my work to require every living part of me, my senses, my soul, my dreams, to flow through me with the power to transform me.

Suddenly, it isn't power or recognition that I want. It is wisdom.

And to know wisdom, I need to know beauty again, and the silence that dwells at its center. I need to touch down into it every day, to draw it up from my own deep sources, to learn its ways and its means of blazing grace into a life, of connecting me to the pro-foundest realities of my being as a woman. And then, I need it to lead me out again in a meaningful work.

My hand grazes a lichen-covered rock. It is velvet and silk, sound and silence, thunder and the sun that continues to roll its gold down upon my head. I turn on my stomach to feel the warmth of the hill against mine, its pulse against mine. I want life to take me in its arms and teach me how to love it again, in the concrete, embodied world of things.

LATER, Mark is grilling steaks just outside the kitchen door. The sun is half an hour above the hill, soft in a sullen, humid spell. Sud-denly, from within, I hear him call in an agitated whisper, "Hurry!"

I do. At the door, I stop. There in the meadow, not five yards from the grazing horses, two young fawns have wandered up to the fence in search of apples.

My heart stops. How could they make themselves so exposed and so vulnerable? All at once, I remember my dream. It was about a woman in a place where fawns would have been safe, at peace, and about a cloth into which a lifetime of wisdom had been stitched into a story of power and coherence and beauty.

I thought of the fantastic confidence of nature. This is the leap of faith, I thought. And I knew that, somehow, all would be well.

2

NOW I AM back home in Boston. My tabletops, bookshelves, and windowsills have become host to a motley of things that I've retrieved from basement and attic. Small pots that I once bought from struggling potter friends. Photographs and prints from my art-student acquaintances. Pens given to me by mentors.

A week after our return, I take out my watercolors and a small tablet of paper and sit in a sunspot on the living-room floor. With a wet brush, I begin to spread rose, coral, and saffron across a page of heavy watercolor paper. Before long, I'm mesmerized by the plumes that bleed in patterns I couldn't have arranged if I'd tried.

As I work, a word leaps to mind.

"Courage," a small voice says.

Courage?

I've always considered myself a person of courage, willing to venture into places and circumstances most people avoid even thinking about. But as I stare at the wet shapes of dream clouds and sunset, forms of sheer mystery, I think perhaps the truth is otherwise. Perhaps I've had courage for the easy things, for situations that didn't involve my own deepest ambiguities.

I put the painting down to dry and lean against the piano. My earliest experiences of beauty centered on this piano. These days, it functions as a glorified piece of furniture gathering dust and overflow books, but once, it stood darkly gleaming in my grand-mother's living room. Back then, it was the family treasure, scrimped and saved for, polished by the scales and études and recitals of my mother's young lifetime by the time I laid eyes on it.

While we waited for Sunday dinner in my grandmother's house, I was allowed to touch the plush of the white keys. My small index finger would balance delicately on the flat bone of them while my mother slid out the bench and, with an emotion I recognized even then as stifled yearning, played a few bars of Brahms or Chopin.

When, a few years later, the piano arrived at our own home, we watched it emerge from the moving truck like a chiseled birth. Proud and polished, it was wheeled gingerly down the ramp, careened on a series of dollies up the rise of the lawn between the twin maples, and rumbled in through the front door as if giddy with the change in atmospherics. A naked wall awaited it. That, and the sticky fingers of four barely civilized children.

Later, after dinner, my mother gathered us in the living room. We sat close together, I the oldest at five. With a hushed reverence that was rare for her, she drew a record out of its brand-new jacket sleeve and set it down on the turntable. In the gathering dusk of a postwar suburban evening, I heard Rachmaninoff's Piano Concerto no. 2 for the first time.

Its triumphant opening chords and its melancholic runs washed over me like a gray and lilac storm, tossing strange and beautiful shadows into the airless room. None of us stirred, least of all my mother. She was lost in a rapture that had softened every dimension of her. I had never seen her as lovely. Her face, her hands, her spirit, all were utterly at rest, drinking in the dark rivers of the adagio as night crept in.

When it was over, my mother's voice joined the currents of dark-ness. "That, children, is the most beautiful piece of music in the world," she whispered.

Without the usual clamor, we went up to bed. As I lay in my room and listened to my little sister drop off to sleep, I heard the first measures of the Rachmaninoff once more. Only this time, it was my mother, alone, playing her piano in the quiet of a summer night.

Shortly after this, I recall making the first thing that I *knew* was beautiful. My mother had enrolled me in the community's junior garden club. On that decisive day, I was given a small clay pot.

Into the pot I stuffed a dwarf African violet. I believe there was also a bit of moss. I imagine—because this I don't remember with any accuracy—that I was advised to tie a ribbon around the arrangement once it was finished.

I loved it.

I was proud. More than that, I was thrilled to discover that I could spend several hours away from my mother and make something that would please her. I didn't even stop to wash my dirt-stained hands; I couldn't ferry my pot home fast enough.

In the dim glow of the kitchen's linoleumed orders, it *was* beautiful. In that curious exchange of the gift without possession—which is perhaps the most apt description of the apprehension of beauty that I know—what I remember most vividly is my mother's voice. Or rather, I remember the *sound* of her voice. Her voice had brightened as if with the thread of a song. Only, she wasn't singing. *Something was singing in her,* pitched as true and unpremeditated as love itself.

It was this song that told me what beauty was, and what it did. It was this song, wrapping me in surprise and pleasure and grace, that opened an unsuspected universe to me. I knew that I wanted its freedom, its vital affirmation with me, always.

Meanwhile, the household grew. Even with a healthy amount of domestic help, my mother's creative time shrank with the arrival of new babies, car pools, lessons, and illnesses. All that she allowed herself was an hour at the piano after we'd gone upstairs to home-work or bed.

And though at first my mother tried to protect me from the domestic shifts and upheavals, I was soon drawn into the norms they required for the orderly functioning of a large household. Free play, improvisational time, neighborhood pick-up theater events, the serendipitous magic of invented games, these had to be cut short for added chores. Play, except when prescribed, became a frill. There were diapers to fold, siblings to watch, younger ones to mobilize in interesting ways. Self-expression became not a virtue to be celebrated, but a drain on the smooth operation of the whole.

Thirty years later, my choice of literature, and writing as my primary means of self-expression, doesn't surprise me. Though like my mother before me, I was expected to fill the late afternoon hours playing Beethoven and Schubert, writing was a language that I came to trust. Writing was silent. It was voice confined in space and time to eminently disposable matter: a few sheets of paper. It required no particular equipment and took up virtually no physical space. Perhaps most tellingly, it was possible to glide with perilous ease between writing as art and writing as industry.

It was during my last year of college that this dual nature came to taunt me. For years, I had swung effortlessly between creative writing, fiction, poetry, and a more polemical feminist journalism. All of these together permitted me a satisfying flexibility that required very little conscious maneuvering on my part. Creative work rose as a simple response to the life around me, every bit as often as did the urge to engage in exposition or argument. But I knew that time would soon demand a choice and a dominant direction—graduate school or a career in journalism. And I knew that this choice would entail more than a simple shift in emphasis.

To which persona was I more firmly attached, the imaginative writer or the journalist? In which did I have the most confidence?

Around this time, I returned home for a visit.

Painting had come into my mother's life by then. Its importance to her, and her seriousness about it, represented a great flowering of self-confidence. Throughout the previous summer, I'd watched her struggle to sustain her classes, to carve out time to work on her canvases. I'd seen her eagerness to talk about them at the dinner table. I remembered the odor of linseed oil, the half-finished canvases drying in the den, and later in the basement. While I was away, I'd taken pleasure in thinking about the calm that settled over her when she had a brush in her hand.

On that visit, however, I was aware that my high-spirited confidence and cant about feminism and freedom were sounding the wrong note. No resting palette was sending its sweet odors upstairs and through the kitchen. The painting had stopped. She had chosen only one work to show for all of those hopes—a basket of spilled strawberries that hung over the piano. The rest: the discipline, the concentration, the time and space demanded to evolve a style and to nurture a vision—all of it was gone, extinguished by motherhood's grueling daily grind. And in the years that followed, it was not to be summoned again.

I returned to campus, disturbed. Though I couldn't have articulated it at the time, I was afraid. I had encountered the image of what I'd risked my life to escape, a life of suppressed talent and compromised dreams.

Linda had reauthenticated beauty for me in profound and, I thought, lasting ways. But now I felt that I had to choose between survival and a more complicated truth—between my ambition and wholeness, between mind and soul—to be taken seriously. Beauty was soft, responsive, vulnerable, at a time when women needed to be powerful, efficient, and competitive. At least until I was more secure, I decided that I needed to keep it at arm's length. And I believed that the stridency of an absolutist feminism would offer this security.

The feminist cause needed writers to debunk many sacred cows, and many times over. We needed to begin telling new stories in order to alter the shape of opportunity as it was experienced for millions of women. Increasingly, I found my time taken up with writing editorials. Being socially useful became more important to me than creating objects of beauty. It would protect me from slipping into irrelevance, the second-rate, invisibility.

This was not a choice of courage, but of calculation and accommodation, I see now. I suspect it is the same one that many women like me made in deference to the times in which we found ourselves.

LINDA CONTINUED to be my "other half." Such friendships are really a state of being. They allow the achieving woman and the creative nurturer to be supported in ways that are quite invisible to the rest of the world, even to husbands and lovers. I know of a lawyer whose best friend makes quilts and home schools her three children, a doctor who relies on her artist sister to arrange and manage the family holidays and rituals. If I occupied the room of my own, Linda cultivated its garden.

Yet as I watch dust motes drift in the morning sunlight along the piano leg, I now see what I was doing. I, and many other women, were simply doing what men have done for generations. We were projecting the disowned or unclaimed parts of ourselves onto others—other women—and expecting them to "carry" those parts for us, to keep them alive for us without our having to take any responsibility, or time away from our careers, to nurture them in ourselves.

I sit up as if I've just been punched in the stomach. How can a woman hope to live authentically unless she is whole? Until she reclaims all her projections, her "sister self" on whom she has leaned all these years, and brings her home again?

To bring beauty home again and to marry it to our purposes, seriously and authentically, whether they be producing widgets or caring for others, *will* require courage—vast doses of it—in a culture whose bottom line is fast and brash efficiency. It will require a rearrangement of our priorities, our concerns, our time, our lives. But what might come to be in us if we can learn to let our souls express their true nature?

I step out onto the deck. My city yard isn't nearly as vast as the landscape that awakened me to beauty two weeks ago. But I have dreamed here too. Beauty isn't a matter of available materials. It is an attitude. It is a tool against the wilderness, around and within us.

I get into the car and drive to the library and head for the art books, plucking them off the shelf like mountain blueberries. Once women married purpose to beauty with a dignity that shaped their cultures. It was inconceivable to them that they would choose between mind and soul, mere survival and creative expression. I crave their arts, the arts of daily life, of folk and craft. I want to surround myself with what was valued less for its aesthetic success than for the way in which it provided the makers' worlds with tools for living that were both useful and beautiful.

I amass as many volumes on Amish quilts and Shaker furniture, Navaho weaving and Adirondack pottery, medieval embroidery and cloister gardens as I can carry. Back home, I lay the books out on the floor and open them, one by one. I have spent so much of my life in a muddle of abstraction. There is a directness in these images that I find as inspiring as Linda's birds' nests and stones. A simplicity of materials, tools, process. Cloth, needle, thread. Wood, saw, sandpaper. Wool and wooden sticks.

I am asking: Can the basic work of my life be made beautiful again? Can beauty, which makes possible in some mysterious way companionship with my deepest self, become the medium of my days, one of the keys to a lost wholeness?

In these images, in the finches' nest, in the polished black stones, I see that I need to part ways with a life that for years has involved me in a view of success and a definition of meaning as a woman that is simply not large enough, or complex enough, to hold all of me. The pot is too small. Or I have been standing in the wrong direction to the sun.

The phone rings.

"Thanks so much for taking care of the house." It is Linda.

"How was your trip?" I ask.

"Fabulous," she replies. "The flowers are happy. I hope you didn't do much work."

"I did a lot of work. Good work."

I pause.

"I've decided to drop the book project."

Until I utter these words, I haven't realized that this is precisely what I have intended to do since the moment I briefly walked clear of doubt and bit into the apple.

Linda laughs.

"I hope this means I'll see more of you?"

I look at my walls, at the books at my feet. I am making a statement here. Taking back a lost piece of my world, setting it in the sun, trying to make it grow. Courage, say the colors of water and fire.

Silence

1

FOR SEVERAL HOURS each morning, I brave my office and
the detritus of an old self. I clear away old paper, to-do lists, outlines, and notes. After about a week of this, the well-worn surface of
my desk reappears, clear as a school girl's in June. In the early
mornings now, I carry my coffee into my study, open my journal,
and wait.

For what, I'm not entirely certain. Any attempt to describe what
began in those hills, or what still stirs in me with restless longing,
runs aground as soon as I try. From out of the stream of epiphanies
that flowed so freely as I sat watching hawks, hours by car from
any phone or deadline, images of a woman transformed, I have
beached on the hard ground of my life as I have known it these
many years.

I write: Where is the self that lies buried beneath two decades of
ambition and professional habit?

I cross out. Begin again.

I need to rediscover the "I" of my deep-in-the-night dreams, of thoughtful letters, of passion, and slow-cooking soup stocks.

My books, the periodicals that line every shelf behind me, stiffen in resistance to this particular line of thought. The jar that holds my pens, my black illustrator's lamp, my dark bottles of ink, these could be the artifacts of a prior occupant, for all the sustenance they provide me now.

For as long as I have written and thought as a grown woman, my office has been my sanctuary, familiar as my blue-flannel nightgown. It has been the "room of my own" where I have struggled to set down truth in words and where I have returned, morning after morning, to find my meaning in this labor renewed. Now, when I need my office to show up in faithfulness because I doubt that I can any longer, I find that it is drained of the qualities that for so long I have taken for granted in it.

Qualities of imagination, warmth, a serene sort of quiet.

AND SUDDENLY I see:

Beneath the silence of concentrated work, my life has no silence.

Beneath the structure imposed by my work, my life has no shape.

I ESCAPE to my car. Through morning traffic, I drive back to the library in Brookline Village, five minutes away. With my canvas bag over my arm, I pass through the metal turnstile and find a seat at one of the empty tables in poetry. For several hours, I take on the protective coloring of books. I leaf through anthologies, skim a monograph on Phoenician boat construction, scribble a note to my agent.

Then I sit. I soak up the purposiveness of the others around me. I remind myself that women wiser and more courageous than I am have walked this territory before me. They've loaded pots and rockers and houseplants into their cars and headed out, to places where they could pick wild berries and catch fish with their hands and not use deodorant or answer to anyone. They've rediscovered the deep meaning of their lives, and happiness, and more than enough that *truly* matters to think and to write about.

They are prophets in a way, a small band who might just help lead me back to where I need to go, since my own resources seem to be failing me. I get up and browse through the card catalog, find several of their books, and head home again.

The mail has arrived. There is not a single manuscript, or check, or personal letter in the lot, just bills and circulars. What, I ask myself, do I think I am doing? I, who have never stopped working, never ceased shaping circumstance and opportunity, making and checking off an interminable to-do list, filling as many hours in the day with my work as has been physically possible (and then some), in contact with a large circle of peers?

I cannot write my way out of this crossroad, or not easily. I cannot use words the way I am accustomed to. I need a new language, one that arises from the silence of the heart.

This is not about "falling" silent. It is about choosing silence as the only valid starting point for genuine self-possession. Silence as an antidote to compulsive overactivity. Silence as a standing still. A taking stock. Silence as a posture of listening, until once again I hear the voice within me.

How do women find the right way to be silent, to stand still? In so masterfully filling the script of our times—achievement, autonomy, power, voice—how many of us left our true inner silence at the stage door or back in the rehearsal rooms of our youth? What calls to us from the silence that we have not heard for longer than we care to remember?

*

THE PHONE doesn't ring. There is no reason for me to rush into my office at daybreak, and as a result, every day, I find less inclination to do so. When I wake, I prefer to remain in bed with my small pile of reading matter beside me.

Insofar as I have any plan at all, it is this. I will take on small writing assignments from editor friends and obtain the rest of what income I need from occasional lectures. I am still earning royalties. Since the day I left college, I have been self reliant. Now I must make peace with temporarily contributing less to our general upkeep than I used to. But I tell myself that I must not let this issue sabotage me. For as much of my day as I can manage it, I need to listen.

Long after my husband is up and showered, I lie watching the patterns that the sun-washed lace curtains make on the spread. Or I open the curtains and watch the wind make great sweeping skirts of the ornamental grasses my neighbor has set into his garden across the street.

Once the front door closes and the car pulls away, my world becomes utterly self-contained, as silent as night. In it at last I let myself feel my exhaustion. My body, which has absorbed all the tension of my taskmaster demands. I am amazed: I had no idea it was even possible to feel such bone-deep fatigue. Bone deep? Soul deep.

I begin to feel the years of pushing release, slowly—drop by drop, it feels some mornings. I try to breathe steadily into the small space that opens inside. It is as if I am resuscitating myself, organ by organ. As if, should I fail to support this disburdening process, I will collapse again into driven efficiency.

Dust motes drift through the sunbeams, the dog stirs and settles, the roses in my lace curtains stencil themselves on the far wall. It is beautiful for no obvious reason. It is beautiful because I feel at peace and still in its presence.

Eventually, I sit up. I open Anne Morrow Lindbergh's *Gift from the Sea.*

On page 51 I read, "Solitude alone is not the answer."

The tidily autonomous woman with a room of her own, a work of her own, will not answer to the claims of authentic selfhood. Not by herself, anyway. A fawn will appear at the door, a dream will linger for weeks, a project will falter.

And then what are we to do? There is life beyond the controlling ego's agenda, no matter how worthy its projects and its "shoulds," and this life lies on the unsettled ground of serendipity, in the seemingly random disturbances in the landscape. They come unbidden. And, if one regards control as a quality of elegance, they come most unbeautifully.

How am I to find the wisdom in this richer, more elusive life — I, who have been too busy to hear my spouse and my friends?

Lindbergh says that we must find and keep a place at the center. We need to learn to "still the soul" even in the midst of our activity. Simply doing so will subtly and over time change us. It will change what matters. What we are able to love and accept in ourselves. What we permit to shape us as people.

And so I breathe. And as I do so, I feel a certain center of gravity returning where fatigue has flowed out, a knowingness that resides in the very surfaces and depths of my resting body. When I am not regarding it as an object to manage, control, keep trim and competently attired, pressed into service or given up to love, I am always amazed at my body's softness. Now that I am no longer dashing to my workout equipment and into the shower before I am even awake, I feel its tenderness beneath the folds of my gown. It gives me a new sense of peace, this communicative tenderness, and so I give it authority to tell me what it needs, what kinds of rest, what waking rhythms, what nourishment.

The center that Lindbergh writes about seems to me to require an analogous softness, an intimate, protected ability to respond to life and to communicate with it on its own terms. I need moments throughout the day, when I can touch down into such softness and receptivity. And *this*, I have only just begun to learn.

It is a little like learning to be a virgin. I get up, bathe, and take the dog for a walk up the hill. In fact, it is much like it, in that beyond these simple rituals, I am utterly at a loss. I don't know where to begin or even *what* I am to begin.

I am keenly aware that if I try and fit myself back into a tidy professional pot too quickly, it will break again, and there is no guarantee that, next time, *I* won't break with it. If the pot that has held my life until now has cracked irrevocably, I need to build a new, more capacious structure, which isn't possible until I know what such a structure must contain.

*

MY FONDNESS FOR pottery may be of help. I've never worked in clay. But I have always admired those who do and have learned a great deal about the art of pottery from reading the early-twentieth-century Japanese potter Shoji Hamada.

Making a pot requires an attitude of reverence. The potter's materials are basic: earth, water, fire, pigment. And because they are basic, each is indispensable. Even the humble twig and the worn rag are honored for their place in the process as ash and ink, soap and surface design. One has to be observant, open, and above all patient with what one has been given. Only in this way can one transform the raw matter of earth into vessels capable of holding meaning, rituals, food, the means of livelihood.

Hamada's pots seem a suitable metaphor for the structure of a life. I yearn for such a metaphor, for a steadying set of practices, a tradition, a set of instructions, as I move into the unknown.

I AM AT my desk on a black morning. Since 8:30, I have spoken barely ten words.

Last night, I dreamed that I was in an underground warehouse. It was a dangerous place, full of documents thrown together at random. My task seemed futile. I was to gather up the few valuable pieces of "my work" and take them back into the world aboveground with me.

From a distance, I caught sight of several of the men who had so successfully sabotaged my painful final months of professional life. I was certain they would stop me if they discovered me. I managed to evade them when, to my horror, not ten feet away, I saw the man who had most effectively thwarted me. He was crouching down too, on his own foraging mission. So we are all rats, I thought.

The meaning of the dream was clear thus far. But then its atmosphere abruptly changed. It seemed that the work I was doing was sacred work. All along, without realizing it, I had been in a monastery. The warehouse was in reality the underground crypt, and surrounding this crypt, like a protective circle of prayer, were the monks' cells.

Now, having discovered the context and the real purpose of my task, I knew that I would go upstairs and into the garden and read poetry.

In the garden, after some time had passed, it was time to attend a small, private funeral. I'd arranged for a Mass to be said in the beautiful chapel abutting the garden and suddenly was distressed to find that the flowers I'd ordered hadn't arrived.

The priest kindly offered me the phone book to dial up the

florist. But instead, I left and returned with my own kitchen bouquet of pink roses.

I DO NOT GROW roses. And until now it hasn't occurred to me that the journey I have commenced may require a burial. To accept the status of a marginal woman, even for a period of time, even for a few hours a day, is perhaps to modify to the point of death the self that has fed too exclusively on the world's ways, its praise, its seductions, its outsized norms of success. This is not what we entered the world of achievement for, and yet it is something that most of us, I suspect, caught like a bad virus, the craving for recognition. To bring forth a new Self, my dream seems to be saying, it is necessary to assume what the culture has taught me to dread more than anything else, a mantle of invisibility, a labor of indirection.

All morning, I have been rummaging in that most private of storerooms, memory. I've pulled out old articles and leafed through old notebooks, trying to revive the younger, more integrated self who once illuminated my steps.

Where has the meaning been? I mean: not just the tapestry of narratives that have flowed into my life and to which I have responded, but those moments that might be said to form a core, a spine of consciousness, that has moved through me into my work and from my work back into my life, instructing, deepening, and enriching over the years.

When was I in communion with more than my striving ego, more than someone else's expectations of my brilliance, more than a victim of my breeding in never being angry, in never—if at all possible—disappointing?

My desk is as littered again with attempts to answer these questions as if I'd not made the effort two weeks ago to set it right. I am going in circles.

I wonder now, as I read my published pieces, what was I looking for?

When I sat in a living room in the slums with a woman who had so many track marks up her arm she looked like a toxic pin cushion, seven days clean of heroin and fighting for every minute of sobriety in order to save her three children?

Or when I stood in the musty hall of a prison talking to a woman who'd murdered her husband?

Or when I spent several days among the prostitutes of Hamburg's sex market, the Reeperbahn, chatting about their other lives as they pulled on their mesh stockings and black boots for the clients who came and went in our midst?

What was I trying to discover in conversations with celebrated women college presidents, feminist psychologists, social activists, poets, spiritualists, and nuns?

I have pursued women and their stories into every conceivable venue, from trailer homes to castles, in labor, in laughter, in death.

Was I looking for some truth that would help me lead a better life? Was I hoping to understand what makes my gender unique in our sensibilities, in our makings and our beings, our healing and our callings?

I wasn't interested in normal, everyday women.

Maybe I assumed that only the feminine experience writ large, archetypal in its heroics and its tragedies, could offer principles clear enough to cut through my own muddle.

I found many answers, many beautiful and poignant stories. But now as I reread them with a clarity that is just dawning, I see that the answers I found weren't *my* answers. They didn't teach me what I needed to hear beneath the din of a busy world. They did not tell me how to live my own life or give me a sense of connection to my soul or provide a vision of how I might grow into wisdom, into a more multidimensional personal reality.

As a result, I became mismatched saucers and worn postcards and tales of small antiques shops in the Adirondacks. I became slides of Chartres (underexposed on account of the clouds that day). I became a worker bee who, drunk on honey and sunlight, cannot possibly begin to understand its own dance.

NOON WAS the hour in the country when I would leave the environs of the stone house and venture down the lane. I'd walk to the lake or take the road out to the pasture and past the barn into the woods for an hour or so. It is noon. I want to leave the unredeeming storeroom of my past and go into the garden. The tall grasses, which I can see from my office window as well as from my bed, beckon. In minutes, I'm under the canopy of maples in my backyard, raking their glorious discards. I bend and sort twigs and bind them in neat stacks. I map out where I might put a few bulbs. I uncover the alpine strawberries, the sweet Nancy and nasturtiums. As I perform these simple tasks, my sense of well-being returns.

For the first time since I've been home, I feel as I did in the country. Perhaps there is another force, a force that has nothing to do with intellectual work, that connects me to my life. Or would, if I placed myself more regularly in its presence.

In my office, I am blocked from true silence. Out here in the garden, my energy and sense of connectedness flow. I lean on my rake and watch bluebirds make forays into the grapes that grow heavy on the trellis. I envy nature its unifying orders, its cycles and seasons. What will it take, what winnowing, what surrenders, to recover my own?

Soon the garden will sleep. I need to buy salt-marsh hay and collect small baskets to cover the young perennials. Before the shadows get much longer, I need to cut back the summer growth so that in February's cold, new buds can form.

Last night, I read that every farming culture in ancient history allowed its land to lie fallow for a season after it had been heavily cropped. Generations of practice had taught that soil, the very ground of being, required a period of rest. It needed to recover what the medieval Anglo-Saxon planters called "heart." Perhaps this is the lesson of silence too.

ONCE I AM back inside, I pull out my mythology book, unread since I was a graduate student, and open to the story of Persephone.

Persephone was the daughter of the corn goddess, Demeter. Life was rich and bountiful for the young Persephone, until the day she went out picking narcissus blossoms alone. Without warning, she was dragged into Hades' underworld kingdom.

Persephone's story is told from Demeter's viewpoint. Demeter was a powerful, established, worldly goddess. She so mourned her lost daughter, and the lost innocence of the instinctive feminine that her child represented, that she refused to allow anything in her power to grow. Life became a barren desert.

But what do we know of Persephone's ordeal? Persephone didn't choose to fall into the underworld. She didn't choose to be penetrated by the shadow-world consciousness. Yet, into its liminal space she went.

Linear time, the time of the world, stopped. Plants ceased to grow. Instead, the heroine entered into a realm in which all time coexists, the truth speaks to the inner self in its own images. Far from the eye of her savvy, image-conscious mother, Persephone discerned (as indeed she had to) those things that would engender a new fertility and a new creativity in the world above. She was on the journey to consciousness.

Persephone needed to make the descent. What she brought back may not have been "useful" in any obvious sense, but it was her truth. She needed to learn what and who she loved, and to own this. She needed to learn a new way of being in the world, of using her hands, her body, her intuition, as she never had before. This was her rebellion.

Isn't it also the journey of love?

Love is always a breaking open, a surrender to a Self one has dimly perceived but which cannot fully emerge until it is seen, made conscious. Perhaps to recover my own deep Self, I must learn to trust again the authority of my own heart. Perhaps I need to retrieve hours and encounters, the moments when I have been open, vulnerable, in deep and silent responsiveness to the love of another.

I have kept the poems sent by J. for several years from his midland winters, and the sporadic postcards dispatched by E. before he appeared, unannounced, at my door hundreds of miles away to propose marriage. But there is no need to open the letters. It is not the lost loves for whom I search, for it is not they who have gone away. It is for she who loved them, in whom desire and recognition burned pure, without smoke; she who, broken out of the distracted, deflecting hours, knew, really knew, what it was to be alive.

I recall a poem of Pound's that I have loved for years.

> And if you ask how I regret that parting:
> It is like the flowers falling at Spring's end
> Confused, whirled in a tangle.
> What is the use of talking, and there is no end of talking,
> There is no end of things in the heart.

Like flowers falling at spring's end, like leaves in autumn. These were the timeless moments of being. But the time came to grow beyond each of them. In the unknowable path of our becoming, these moments were meant to break in order for us to move into another stage of the journey. It is in the nature of all beauty, all art, and all craft that they be strewn with beautiful fragments, artifacts. Why do we ever imagine that our lives ought to be different? Even the garden, even in its season of silence, teaches this lesson. The task of love, like the potter's task, is to preserve in consciousness the essential materials, the words, the poems, one's dreams.

These are arts of indirection and of approximation. There are days of grace and days of toil. This is the way change creeps into our lives most of the time, I imagine. We continue to put in our time, make the journey from shower to desk. Then one day, a free moment begins to be filled with something different. A new music, an inner conversation. I ponder, as I look back on the tidied yard, where I might plant a rose.

2

MY BROTHER IS DEAD.

Last night the phone rang. It was my mother.

"Tim is dead."

My brother, dancing somewhere above the Manhattan night, thirty-five, beautiful, brilliant, crazed, is dead. Details are murky. It looks like murder. Or did he commit suicide? An accident, the police are saying.

Accident. On a dark and rainy midnight, my brother fell five stories to his death in the dark wedge between two rooftops on the Lower East Side, apparently having failed to see the gap.

I AM MUTE, numb to everything but the slivers of what feels like glass breaking open every vein in my body.

The violence, of course, hasn't ended. There is his wife, having to identify his mangled body. There is the hovering, shattered presence of the other, younger brother, with whom Tim and his wife made a frequent trio. And there is the disconnected, impossibly unsatisfactory narrative of what actually happened.

Tim was the funniest and one of the most insightful men I have ever known. He was also one of the most isolated and tortured. A competitive swimmer, his lithe six-foot-three frame cut the water like a cool, incandescent flame. He was a metal sculptor and artist who once thought of becoming an architect, but like me, felt the relentless pressure to be successful and eventually traded his wild, beautiful dreams for mutual-fund management—for "securities."

Then, there is the other story of Tim. The drugs and the booze craziness with friends at his upper-middle-class suburban high school, ducking out of classes, skirting the police, playing with his life as if it truly were an inextinguishable flame.

Icarus. By the time he graduated high school, three of his closest friends were dead. What did he do in later years with all that loneliness, grief, and guilt? All we know now, among the many things that we are discovering, is that he never mentioned their names to his wife. Not once.

NOTHING IS without association, not even the unrelenting white and gray landscape of upstate New York that flows beneath the plane in lovely patches as we fly west to be with his body; quilts of farms, of human industry, an order stitched out of the years, hewn in rocks and back-breaking labor.

We arrive. Everyone is just as we are, dazed. Mute. My father is vacant and shattered. M.'s family, elegant European Jews, cannot even speak. For the sake of grief itself, they try to respect the oddities of the Catholic funeral rite. They stand as we all do for hours at the wake as more than five hundred people pass through. People from countless walks of life. People we've never met but with whom Tim had once formed a bond and who have loved him ever since. This was Tim. No one ever merely liked Tim. They loved him.

At the graveside, beautiful, demonically grieving M. stumbles about in a pair of silver hiking boots. I will never forget those boots. They are the most elegant statement anything could possibly have made to the senselessness. I'm sure that Tim was with her when she bought them. Perhaps they were his Christmas gift to her. He would have loved to know that she wore them on this occasion. Hadn't they taken a Rhode Island Red rooster into their SoHo loft as a pet? Hadn't he once convinced a landscaper that he knew how to drive a truck, only to dump three tons of manure in the middle of a downtown intersection? This, all of this, was Tim.

HOME AGAIN. Only now in the silence can I stitch my grief and begin to heal. Mother sends along copies of Tim's wedding pictures. M. in her lavish gown, Tim beside her in tails at the Lotus Club. M. offering Tim her hand. Immediately, I tuck them into a folder I've begun. They are too painful to look at.

As I stare into the bleak winter landscape, a different image comes to me. Tim and I are walking, separately and alone, through city streets not our own. The quality of light could be that of Philadelphia or Baltimore, New York or Chicago. It sometimes seemed that when we weren't thinking or writing, we spent all the mornings from eighteen to twenty-five doing this in one form or another. We wanted to know the world and at the same time to defend ourselves against it—defend our authenticity, newly discovered, from intrusion, or betrayal, or compromise. I suspect that most of us who grew up in the sixties and seventies, men and women alike, explored a similar terrain of exile. We were experimenting with ways to keep the Self alive in a culture that has no reverence for silence.

Wet pavements, chilly dawns, black trees slick with rain, coffee from station urns, a cigarette and a book to avoid the glances of strange men—these were the stations of our youthful journeys.

It never occurred to us, particularly as women on the cutting edge of our ambitions, that in living this way, we were establishing a fatal divide between who we really were and what we permitted as acceptable realities. The face one showed the world protected and at the same time obscured the deep Self. This became a way of being, a way of occupying one's place in the world.

And so we fell into the world of noise. It seemed just one of the inevitabilities of modern life that we did nothing to oppose. I became the detached journalist, a cipher for other people's stories, for one-sided secrets. Life spoke, and I listened, without my having to give much in return.

The hidden lie in all of this was that I thought of myself as being disciplined, responsible, purposeful, only keeping up a certain number of necessary boundaries in order to do my work well. I was more concerned with doing than with being. I didn't take time for reverie or reflection. I didn't see that my work had become less a statement of my values than of my relation to a persona, the name on the title page, a substitute for the deep, original Self that had grown detached and mute.

I now believe it was in the face of this reality that Tim drank. The years, the reeling years, seemed as if they might go on forever. In and out of jobs, business school, recovery programs. Until seven years ago, when he stopped all the madness, put on an expensive suit, and walked to his office on the thirty-third floor of the World Trade Center every day. He was a portfolio manager with dreams of running his own mutual fund. No one among his Wall Street colleagues knew anything about the road he'd traveled to get there.

THROUGH THE LENS of my brother's life, I see the price we pay for accepting life in the fast lane. It is an essential isolation, which eventually leads to a loss of the center that Lindbergh writes of. Without this center, we aren't the people we are meant to be, just a bundle of reactions and defenses and biases and opinions. We have no memory and no true, guiding silence.

I do not believe that I have lived my life without integrity. But I would say that in a period of history shot through with the language of power, of assertion, of doing, I and most of the women I know have been sufficiently distracted by the thing we call "success" to have cut ourselves off from the quiet search among the images of our own silence for the works, the life, that might grow from them.

I have never seen this so clearly as I do today, as a choice that we make about our way of being in the world.

As a woman, I see now that I must exercise the other choice and occupy the different place to which it leads me.

3

THE SNOW IS thick around the base of the trees.

I put out sunflower seed for the cardinals, watch my breath pull into little clouds against the cold, and set out.

Before leaving the city for Tim's funeral, I called a priest whose sermons I had heard on occasion in the past. Sam listened as I paced, wept, talked, and paced some more. Finally, he said to me, "Pray for Tim."

This seemed preposterous.

"But he's dead!" I responded angrily. "How do you pray for someone who is no longer alive?"

"You'll find the way," he answered quietly.

A Mass is in progress in the seminary chapel downtown. I slip into one of the last rows and let the familiar words and rhythms wash over me. More than the ritual, I find myself attracted to the stones. In the candlelight, they have the soft patina of bone or sand, reminiscent of the ancient Romanesque churches that I love dotting some of the hillsides of Europe. The raw materials of a culture and a faith—if not mine any longer, or not at this moment in any particularly engaged sense, mine by dint of the echoes of childhood. I am grateful for their presence.

The Mass ends. The candles on the altar are being extinguished, the few lights put out. Suddenly the male voices begin to chant:

Non Nobis Domine, sed tibi, Domine Gloriam.

The lamentation fills the now empty nave. And all at once, I find myself paralyzed by the power of my grief. It feels as if Tim is here with me, coming toward me through the music.

I can hear the strains of the tenor voices. I can hear my own erratic breathing. Tears are running down my face. As the chant continues its rounds, the pain that has physically wracked my body since he died, gradually, miraculously, is lifted. I am in a state of perfect, complete silence.

And in the place of pain in the back of this darkened church on a bitter cold February day, I find myself holding a vision of childhood, of the Canadian shoreline where we grew up and were both exquisitely happy.

After the long winters with their many activities, after school sports, student council, and ballroom dancing, the Canadian summers were our salvation. Time was replaced by simplicity—an emptiness so rich and organic that it allowed the Self to find its shape and hear its voice in its vast proportions, and thus to enter fully into the graceful unfolding of its days.

This was the silence of our childhood, Tim's and mine. A world not of our own making, but our most cherished inheritance.

Life was rooted in the cycles of nature: the seasons, the tides, the day's demands for work and food, the night's for rest. The Irish and Scots who settled there built stone walls and tidy cottages, grew peaches and cherries, corn and grapes, painted, danced, raised their children and their flowers.

It was a world of profound interdependence, charity—and silence. Silence was its center, its organizing principle. And here we found ours. In the shifting play of tide and light on the broad plain of the changing sea, I felt myself to be in continuous presence of the holy. Birds, their flights and shadows, the reeds and stones, the dirt roads, the scattered offshore farms with their long acres of corn and wheat braked by towering elms—in these, I heard what C. S. Lewis once called "the echo of a tune we have not heard, news from a country we have never yet visited."

Here we were led by the hand of nature's creative force, an order in which we learned—for that sweet, suspended time of childhood, at least—to trust that we would be kept safe on the verge of life's terrible isolations.

IN THIS PLACE of prayer, I have been led back to a treasure beneath brokenness. One of the names of home.

I walk to the car and make my way back home. I cannot go back to the world of childhood. I can't bring Tim back to life. But I can learn from the first and forgive the world the second. I can learn again the detachment that allows for a passionate attachment to the right things. I can reclaim the virgin heart that waits in silence, open to encounter, to being filled and spilled, astounded and broken and made new again, in the transformations of earth and flesh, water and fire.

The days become weeks, and the weeks soon make up a month, and I feel the silence working in me as a mending and a grace.

I HAVE DISCOVERED a two-mile trek that starts at the end of my lane. It crosses over wooded hills and the back side of conservation land before it ends on a ridge overlooking a small farm. I take it most days now after I write and before I begin dinner.

My feet break twigs that lie in my path. Occasionally, I hear a squirrel not far away. But mostly I listen to the silence. These walks become a way of holding something sacred in present time; they are a practice of daily silence. I move between the depths of memory and the beauty that offers itself to exploration here.

From out of this hellish time, words have begun to take on a whole new life. I write to friends who've sent beautiful letters about Tim or their own stories of loss. Letters become a way not just of listening, but of digging into the inarticulate and learning to share. I try to tell the story of these past few months, about the new place of silence in my life. I try to use words in the service of silence, to describe a vision of the self mediated by the occasional brush with mystery. About the gifts of memory and nature, and of those known places that share much with the experience of human love as they open us to deeper insights into the Self, to glimpses of hidden harmonies between our work and our affections. More than anything, I try to connect.

I am satisfied that for now this is enough. What matters isn't the specific form my work will take come the spring, but my continuing engagement with the silence. From this, the life and the work will arise.

4

WHEN I RETURN from my walk today, I take down a small collection of books that I have kept above my desk for many years. Slender as volumes of poetry and sharp as teeth, they have waited like untouched totems, and with them the memory of a woman I have never forgotten and the afternoon that I spent with her long ago before a fire in a rose-scented room.

Fog thickened to stew the chill November rain that afternoon as I trudged up College Hill toward the green. It enveloped me as I stood waiting at the door of Number 9.

I'd developed a fascination with the French writer and diarist Anaïs Nin when I ought to have been doing many other things the fall of my senior year. And now I was going to tea with a retired member of the English faculty who had made herself something of an expert on the subject.

When Marianne Brock pulled open the door and burst into laughter, I knew at once that I was in the presence of some dervish or deva. She was a not wholly self-governed force. A kind of vibration, almost a humming sound, emanated from deep inside her, reducing her floral dress and good English talc to a poor variant of flat champagne. She was something mineral, like a shooting star, uncomposed in all but the one sense that propelled her being.

She ushered me up the stairs and into a parlor where a fire blazed in the grate. Tea had been set and books lay next to the cups. She settled herself into a yellow loveseat, and, without the usual introductory gropings, began. "I thought I would go mad in this godforsaken town, after Oxford."

It immediately occurred to me that it was Marianne Brock, her being, rather than the subject of her knowing, that I needed to undertake on this visit to discover.

Somerville College, 1930. Her brilliance seen even then

(though she did not say this) halfway across the world, in Winnipeg. After Oxford, Paris beckoned. The Paris of Picasso and Pound. And Henry Miller. Somehow or other the irrepressible Marianne Brock fell into this fabled world. She wrote poems with them. Did she work at one of the art presses that were so prolific? That she was an intimate, after an hour with her, I had no doubt. But then, the war came. Or perhaps none of this in the end satisfied. In any event, she fled Paris and Europe for the tail of the American Rockies.

At twenty, I was enchanted. I already knew that I needed to achieve the best solutions my generation of women had devised for our entry into mainstream professional culture. This was the separate self, the self who transcended the terms of origin, geography, even of education and social expectations, to answer the call of achievement and personal freedom.

But Marianne Brock, seated in the flesh before me, was handing me the gift of the possible. The restless search for the *rightness* of experience, a gathering of days composed into an unrepeatable, original flow of works and relationships—this was the life that until that moment I'd only allowed myself to dream.

How lovely it would be to change one's point on the map at will, move to a houseboat (literal or otherwise), and from there strike out—unattached and free—into the life around one.

I returned to my room with my arms full of Marianne Brock's personal copies of Nin's novels. From the dining room downstairs, I heard the distant clatter of knives and the laughter of common mortals. I felt no urgency to join them. I set the books on my rug like a cairn and sat cross-legged in front of them, so that I could watch the obscure and final strokes of that hidden, remarkable day glide into night.

Soon my wanderings began.

At the end of the following spring, I left my room with its drafty windows. I walked into the sunlight casting all sorts of illusions in front of me. Like Marianne Brock, I found many moons hung in many places on a multitude of maps.

It didn't concern me that afternoon so long ago that by the time I met her, Marianne Brock had made another choice. She had brought her spirit to rest amid the gentle slopes of the Connecticut River Valley, her wanderings ceased.

I didn't wonder, twenty years ago, about the conversion, the inner transformation, that had brought and kept her close to a simpler and more grounded life.

It has taken me twenty years to realize that the real gift Marianne Brock gave me that day was this: In orienting herself not by the genius of her ambition, but of her deep self, she had never ceased to name, and to *rename*, the life that was right for her. After years of wandering, Marianne Brock decided that she needed to set down roots and to live in context, in deep relationship, not just as a busy professional, but as an observer and maker of beauty, as a lover.

This inward-turning journey didn't lead to diminishment or to a withdrawal from the world or to failure. To the contrary, it led to a life of passion and focus and integrity.

She became a brilliant professor of poetry. And, well after the time in life when it was the proper thing to do, she fell deeply in love. She taught poetry, and she loved a man who too loved poetry, and she never stopped burning in those loves. I know this because when I met her at seventy and she had lost the man of her life, she incandesced still.

After years of thrilling, buoyant, scandalous "freedom" as one of life's apprentices, she became one of its masters. She had integrated passionate engagement with detachment in a way that meant something and gave her her real power as a woman and as a human being.

And finally, in old age, she'd become an innovator. She discovered in herself a language of hospitality and generosity from which she could build a fire and offer an unknown young woman a cup of tea; through the wisdom of her own life, a map for her soul.

This is the other way, the way of silence. Silence makes the ravishing wildness and the hidden orders articulate, as beauty, as form, as sustainable life. Silence brought what she had lived, seen, and felt into the crucible of reflection and held it there in a sort of vital fixity until its meaning could be distilled. Only then could she express it in words and actions, in a meaningful life.

I NEVER RETURNED Marianne Brock's books, and this careless lapse shamed me for years, until I began to suspect that somehow she had intended this too.

Now I replace them on the shelf and go down into the living room. I turn on all the lights and, for the first time all winter, I build a fire.

The task of midlife entails entering the silence daily, tending it, and waiting, for the sake of the deer, the wild apples, the wildness in one's soul, and when they appear, holding them close as the treasures that they are. They are the texts of our future journeys, the soul revealing its own wisdom.

While the fire takes, I go into the kitchen and get the porcelain cup that I bought in Paris when I was very young. While the water boils for tea, I look at the collection that in time grew up around it. In porcelain and bone china, in glass and crude clay, these cups once represented to me a vision of connection. They were not a hope chest, exactly, but the equivalent of other girls' silver or first samplers; all of them symbols of a hospitality that we gathered like eager squirrels, imagining a life very different from the ones in which we found ourselves, in which even as simple and human an impulse as hospitality would prove a complicated affair, full of the tensions of assertion and compromise.

I bring in the tea, set it down beside the warm light of the fire, and look at it closely. Can I allow the silence and receptivity of a teacup to become once again a vital symbol for my life? A cup is a necessary vessel. Its value lies not only in its strength and beauty, but in what it holds. Not only in what it holds, but what it gives away. Infinitely contained, infinitely generous. Perhaps this is the story of the life that is shaped by silence.

Fertility

1

THIS WEEK the seed catalogs began to arrive. Page after page of flowering bulbs, banks of midseason blossoms, lilies, hostas, and roses tempt me to transform my humble pachysandra beds into a small, city Eden.

I begin dreaming of a garden. I want to grow rosemary and basil, pick mint that I can use for tea. I want a beautiful, functional, meditative retreat. I want color, fragrance, and the revitalizing qualities of manual work to balance my writing life.

I am learning to listen with my heart now that my days are more full of silence, and I find that the old traditions are speaking to me with renewed freshness. I've pulled out an old quilt and laid it on our bed. I've found a few balls of blue mohair and a skein of hand-painted merino, remnants from old scarf projects, and placed them in a basket for inspiration. And now, a garden.

I am willing to risk a new connection to "women's work," because I suspect that there are new ways in which my private creative time might bring some long-buried richness to my professional work. A woman's creativity may well be her most potent tool for expressing a new sense of authenticity. On my little patch of earth, no more than a quarter acre of shady, substandard lawn, I am free to do what I do for my own satisfaction. This fulfills me in ways that I can't explain and don't intend to.

My garden will never be as glorious as Linda's, say, or Katrina's. For one thing, I haven't the room. For another, I can't imagine sacrificing as much of my time as their grander schemes demand.

But the point of my garden will be different as well. It will serve as a delicate reminder that creativity is never purely cerebral. It is erotic. It demands what the medievals called "heart"—the life force that dwells in the "nowness" of beauty and in the "hereness" of passionate participation.

I don't remember where I learned to plot a garden on graph paper. But I begin making sketches, notes on color, growing times and conditions, light requirements. At noon, I descend on the local copy shop in the village, arms loaded down with gardening magazines, blueprints for path formations, lists of plants for silver gardens and edible salads. I hurry home and paste these in the garden journal that has begun to occupy my early morning hours. I tape pictures of plants that I covet on the kitchen wall and in my study, at eye level with something that I've read in the last few weeks:

"Existential authenticity occurs when we step beyond static patterns into the pursuit of creative projects." (Keller, 14)

AFTER BREAKFAST, I dig a semicircular bed behind the garage. The first cuts are the easy part. For the next four hours, I haul away rocks the size of grapefruits until my shoulders ache and I am running with sweat.

Doubtless, the afterlife of stones is a richer soil. I'm certain that their chalk and lime, broken down, make any dirt worthier of the higher life forms, the rhododendron and apples, that will grow there. I just haven't anticipated the struggle to break through to open ground. Years ago, I'd put voluntary suffering, physical or psychic, into the hatbox of rejected femininity. Down it went, along with the obligatory cupcakes for school fairs. Martyrs no more, I vowed. Now here I am, embracing it.

Physical work.

Unremunerated work. So be it.

When the day is over, I take a stroll over to the neighboring farm. It too is being readied for its acres of corn and broccoli, tomatoes and beans. Tractors sit low among the rough furrows, trimmed fruit boughs lie in heaps by the side of the road. Soon my quarter acre will reclaim a lost kinship. I am moved by this in ways that I don't pretend to understand.

My life now is seriously pared down. On the level of daily routine, this feels incredibly good, cleansing and simplifying. We are doing more with friends at home, going out less; we're relying on last year's clothes and simpler gifts and more vegetarian meals.

The quality of being in a more natural, unfolding sense of time is very good for me creatively. Without the future pressing in with its deadlines and its voices of the new, there is space to move. There is integrity. I've brought down from the attic a novel that I abandoned three years ago and with it several unfinished stories eked out one summer against the impending pressure of the last book project. Now I have the time to look at these projects, and the right kind of energy as well.

Yesterday was idyllic. I wrote, revised a story, did some needlework, and walked with the dog until it was six o'clock. In the evening, I read.

*

TODAY IS our anniversary. The sun is bright in a clear sky, the temperature fifty-four degrees—perfect for the grass we planted on Saturday. The beds are still covered with straw, the new plants put in and fertilized, the bird feeders full of thistle and sunflower. Quite a transformation, in one short month!

After these many years and changes in the intensity level of our time together, even in the directions of our work, Mark continues to teach me about patience, about holding my tongue, about the virtue of doing something just because it is the right thing to do, whether or not one's emotions are along for the ride. And I believe that I have taught him a few things about courage, risk, passion, and freedom.

For the first hour of the day, I worked on sketches from a book of Frank Lloyd Wright's designs. Then we went into town for a breakfast of pancakes and strawberries.

As we walked back into the house, the phone rang.

It was the medical lab, calling to tell me that I am pregnant.

2

THE LAND OF my childhood comes back to me in a flood of desire; the old farmsteads and the barns, the gentle orders of home. Every cell in my body longs to be by water.

I can't return to Canada. But I *can* go to the place that most closely resembles it for me and that over the years has claimed a similar place of my heart, the fishing cove of Menemsha on Martha's Vineyard.

Mark has responded to the news with a whir of masculine activity. After running out to purchase what he considers the essential equipment for early pregnancy—a new pair of cross-trainer sneakers and a cappuccino maker—he sneaked out yesterday to ogle baby strollers. Every five minutes, he inquires about my bowel movements and otherwise moons about.

I am not much better. I'm assailed alternately by fear and fantasy. Am I moving too quickly? Has the life inside already ended, as they have before? My state of mind is that of amorphous and universal tenderness. I have no ambition except to share a sofa, lie on the beach, feel sand running through my fingers.

"I need to be by the water," I tell him.

He agrees. It'll be a good hour down there if he can focus his mind on the baseball practices or golf.

*

EVERYTHING SMELLS of ocean here: the white sheets, the white towels, the faded deck furniture. One can taste it on the breeze.

After we unpack the groceries, I go upstairs and meditate. Below me is the water, and just beyond, the Elizabeth Islands.

This certainly wasn't the journey I'd envisioned standing on a hillside in the country several months ago. I hadn't had in mind a complete change of state.

I feel so accompanied. So companioned. This is amazing to me. I always expected pregnancy to feel like an occupation by some alien force. It is more like the communion of lovers, the dialogue is so palpable.

MARK HAS GONE off on his bike for a few hours. I read desultorily, make a few sketches, and watch small black migratory birds rove in great clustering clouds from tree to tree. When I tire of this, I take a short walk to the beach down through the low-growing trees, collecting shells and leaf specimens as I go. A spot of scarlet on the ground, an egret rushing out of the marsh grass, any gratuitous beauty, moves me to tears.

I find a perch on a dune just above the high surf, pondering a line from a book I read this morning. A *Very Close Conspiracy* by Jane Dunn, it is a study of the relationship between Virginia Woolf and Vanessa Bell.

"Resistance to the mother, Jung argued, resulted [too] in a daughter's developing her intellect for the express purpose of breaking the mother's power," Dunn writes.

The author was referring to Virginia. But as I watch the gulls bicker over a clam, I think, wasn't this precisely the subtext of my generation? Even if we weren't in resistance against our personal mothers (and many of us were), we were appalled and repelled by the selfless, nurturing archetype of "the mother."

Like everyone I knew, my mother stayed home and saw to our care, our meals, our happiness. The family *was* my mother's great ongoing project. Creativity was in the details, and she put enormous energy into them. She would surprise us with guessing-game days, pack riddles into our lunches. She loved to open the living room of the summer house to evening bingo games or neighborhood root-beer parties. Sundays were reserved for family charades, cards, and drives out to the country in search of old cider mills and flea markets.

But around the family dinner tables of those suburban fifties and sixties, the ground rules were changing. Our parents nurtured in us the dream of public achievement, the satisfactions of thinking big thoughts, rather than tripping over the minute details of the nursery. Even if they hadn't read *A Room of One's Own*, they were raising us to be worthy of the Bloomsbury pair. I'm not sure whether they thought about the potential conflict that might ensue if we were then confronted with the same biological conditions as our mothers.

One memory comes to mind that illustrates the ambivalence those years produced. When I was seventeen and in Paris, my classmates and I were invited to the home of a couple whose daughter attended the Parisian sister school to ours.

In threes and fours, we ascended the gilt lift to their flat in the posh sixteenth arrondissement. In discreet pairs, we were offered ripe cheeses and foie gras and stuffed meat puffs. We discussed Molière, the museums, Rodin's studio. A maid passed small exquisite tarts and petits fours brighter and more beautiful than any we'd seen in the patisserie windows. Since I was still involved in my starvation regimen, I refused them all. When the daughter, Sonia, gravitated to where I was sitting, somewhat apart, I asked if I could be shown to her bathroom scale.

She took me through her parents' bedroom, into their lavish private bath.

"Have you stopped menstruating?" she asked in breathless, impeccable English.

I nodded, slipped out of my shoes, and stepped up on the pink scale.

Sonia peered over my shoulder.

"That's not enough!" she gasped.

From the distant living room, we could hear the sounds of young laughter, the mannerly overtones of the adults.

But no one had come for us. And we suddenly found that we had no interest in returning. We sat in the bathroom and talked for the rest of the evening, and by the time I had to leave, had become close friends.

At one point, lowering her voice, she said to me in a worldly, maternal voice, "You must be careful. I've heard that after this kind of thing women can have difficulty bearing children."

Children?

I was quietly stunned. That this sophisticated and highly intelligent young Parisian woman regarded childbearing as de rigueur . . . !

Like her, I attended a private girls' convent school under the tutelage of nuns whose task it was to "finish" us. But in all of my years there, in all my years in a large family and in the large families of my friends, no one had ever spoken to me about my future as a mother. An artist, yes. An intellectual, yes. But children? It was a French thing, I concluded.

In college where I arrived only months later, children were never discussed. Looking back, I realize that resistance to the mother was present in nearly everything we thought, read, and did. The women whose works we admired—Woolf, Georgia O'Keeffe, Gertrude Stein, Anaïs Nin, Emily Dickinson—were either childless or had so buried their identities as mothers that motherhood seemed to bear no relation to their real, "creative" work—nor, hence, to our views of them. Our own ideas about a creative life evolved in the long nights we spent at the library or in the art studio.

But by far the most dramatic resistance to motherhood was evidenced in our choices about motherhood itself. How could we hope to live like Virginia Woolf or Anaïs Nin if we were hobbled by the tending of babies and the changing of diapers, decorating holiday cookies and ferrying prepubescent youngsters to dance classes? Almost every woman I knew was having college or graduate-school abortions. We did them for the most part with a tight-lipped invincibility. The object was to avoid at all costs diverting ourselves from the exercise of our intellectual powers.

Once we entered the world of men, we began to hide our pregnancies and minimize the caretaking pressures of sick children, calling in sick ourselves rather than appear too "feminine" and therefore unfit for the job.

Now I am with child. A world of possibility, as wide as the sea, opens before me, and as I sit watching the water, I realize how grateful I am for what I received as a young girl. I loved the unhurried hours in the garden, along the shore, my mother's hand in mine. I am grateful for the energy she put into making our household a creative and peopled place. I am grateful that I did not have to struggle against the subliminal ambivalence my generation bears toward mothering, for even given such a generous childhood, the road was not smooth.

How different is the world my child is being born into! She will enter a world that is not family centered, not even particularly child friendly. Into a world of adults—women and men alike—who are deeply conflicted about giving too much of ourselves "away" in the selflessness my mother's life represented to us. Who are, like me, not even very competent at nurturing themselves in the ways that really matter.

Perhaps the next step on our collective journey as women is to re-envision the creativity, the eros, so implicit in giving life. Is there a way to reclaim the fertility, the richness of heart and soul that arises from the mundane work (and play) of nurturing a child?

I certainly want to share with my child my love of the shore . . . Won't this nurture me as much as her?

I want her to know the wonders of making, of painting, gardening, music . . . Won't this enable *me* to be more creative again?

I certainly want to try and protect her from having the terrible experience of alienation, the profound sense of incompleteness, that I have known . . . How can I do this unless I model for her the balance and the wholeness that come from a healthy sense of self-worth?

To mother well, a woman must give birth not only to a child but to a new Self, a Self that goes well beyond the straightforward persona of the successful professional. We didn't realize this (or didn't want to face it) back in the years when our first priority was to create those successful professional selves. Perhaps the time has come now, and perhaps among mothers who at midlife have achieved the first kind of success, to begin the project of imagining what an evolved, restored, maternal creativity might bring to *all* of our works, private and public.

I stand and stretch. My whole being feels like a plant reaching for the light these days. I am certain of two things. The first is that there ought to be no conflict whatever between being a mother and being a force in the world. The second is that, restored to ourselves, we can create our own paradise. As I head back to the inn, I spot a small granite-colored stone with two bands of striation unbroken continuously around it—a double lucky stone. A good omen, and a good emblem of the afternoon's thoughts.

JUST BEFORE DAWN I wake, pull one of Mark's sweaters over my nightgown, and creep down to where I keep my writing materials in a canvas bag by the fireplace. An inner voice has roused me, and I move quickly so as to keep up with it. I bring a glass of water to the table, light the candle left there from dinner, and begin to write.

Words and images spill onto pages that multiply without effort under my pen. I haven't written with such abandon since I was twenty and in love. I lose all awareness of time and place, of the unresolved questions that await me back home.

I write and write, unable to separate myself from the process sufficiently to know what the words are even "about." They seem to be stories, or fables, written in a fairly symbolic language. I simply set down what asks to be put down.

After countless minutes, my hand begins to ache from the intensity of the effort. I stop to rest and see that the candle has burned all the way down and is about to go out. Light has begun to infuse the gray October morning. I hear Mark on the stairs.

He comes and wraps me in a blanket and forces me to lie down on the sofa. It is a fine and good thing that he does so, for I am tired by now.

And I know what I need to know. My words are coming back to me from a long-dead and secret place, a language that speaks as much through my body as my mind. As I lie on the sofa, I understand in a way that remains obscure but is absolutely alive, that a new creative life is stirring in me and that it will arrive with the same power and uncompromising demands as the child with whom my future is now irrevocably joined.

✲

BACK HOME, I pace in the garden.

There are many things to consider in the matter of a garden. But the most important is patience. The roses and peonies I've ordered won't come until April. The same with the astilbes and the miniature lily. Even if I were to plant a few hostas now, they wouldn't bloom for nine months. A garden can't be hurried.

Michael has put in two ten-hour days, regraveling the driveway and laying large fieldstones back to the new bed. Now the path is finished. It wends along a bed of white gravel past the garage to the rose trellis and from there to the back lawn. It is beautiful, simple, grave in its variegated grays. Where it ends, I can take a few steps into the garden proper and there follow a few smaller stones to my "hidden" spot, nestled behind a bank of rhododendron and hydrangea. A small terra-cotta terrace waits there, a mere three by five feet wide.

Seated with my journal, entirely hidden from view on this small terrace, I am at peace, free to meditate in the open air, free to read and think and write. Free to hear a new and unfamiliar voice, as the sun warms the stones beneath me, a voice that says, Care for yourself, take time, take pleasure, listen to the leaves, listen for God . . .

At times, I worry at what seems a lack of motivation.

I go to see Mrs. W. I tell her about the quietude I'm experiencing, bordering on lethargy.

She replies that maybe I am not in a lull at all (the word I'd used) but am finally entering a more natural state of being than the frenzy that has dominated my life for so many years.

At first, I resist this. I put up a few good arguments. As usual, she simply smiles and remains silent.

Home again, I make a cup of green tea and suddenly remember last night's dream. I was somewhere in the "south." I think it must have been a Caribbean island. I was traveling with a group of wonderful, loving people, and when at last I had to leave, I found myself being embraced by them. Several of the men, island dark and beautiful, lifted me up on their arms into the air like a bird. Then one of them brought me close to him and whispered into my hair, "You will come back."

I woke suffused with the warmth of the islands, their sensuality, their sun and fruit and languor. I felt an unimpeded relation to the earth and sea. Color and vividness poured through me, and I swam in it joyfully.

Now, over breakfast Mark talks about inventing the perfect toaster, then the perfect alarm clock. I'm jotting down ingredients for his beef stew while I slather strawberry jam from North Carolina on my carrot muffin—the jam a gift from Sara's sister who joined our dinner party here the other night. Later, I will pot a few pansies.

A woman's creative life is a question of rhythms, of pacing, of seasons. Part of our task is learning to respect them. My dream wasn't about decorative touches. It was about a way of being that seems to be summoning me.

3

LINDA AND S. HAVE invited us to the country for the weekend
and we've happily accepted. The roads through Connecticut are
damp with ice melt. As we drive west under low, gray skies a feeling
of intense privacy seems to enfold us. It will be a quiet time
together.

I have needed to see Linda's face, just as I know that she has
needed to see my body. We have both been childless for so long
that it had come to feel like a mutual, unstated compact. Now I
have changed all that. What place will she make for this fact
between us?

SHE IS WAITING at the heavy door of the hut, huge with welcome. Immediately, she has to see me. She holds me at arm's
length, turns me to the side, and then around, a full 180 degrees.

"You're still so small," she concludes with disappointment.

I'm not sure what she expected.

"But look—." I flatten my shirt around the growing drum of my
belly. "I've gained twenty pounds already!"

She is skeptical. "You still don't weigh as much as I do."

We laugh.

"And I have something to show you."

She pulls at the hair stick that has been holding her topknot in
place. Down tumble her beautiful lengths of sable hair, laced now
with gray.

"I've decided to stop coloring."

"You look beautiful," I say, and kiss her.

She cocks an eyebrow.

"Dignified."

We sit down to a cup of tea while the men go off to read. I can see that she is delighted with me, with my condition, with my health, with my happiness. But I also feel, ever so slightly (or is it my anxiety?), that the condition of her delight is a new and subtle detachment. As if she has taken a half step back, the better to see me.

She's just finished another issue of the magazine and is in the postdeadline exhaustion I know so well. We talk about the office characters whom I also know, those who thwart her obsession with timeliness, those who make short shrift of her passion for grammatical purity. The afternoon begins to meld into so many we've shared over the years. We build a fire, take Charles for a walk, and start to make dinner.

It is only when we do so, pouring out oil and chopping and kneading pizza dough, that I realize this may very possibly be the last time we will ever spend in this way, alone with our talk and our thoughts. I am saddened.

"What are you going to do about work once the baby is born," she asks, at this very moment.

"I'm not sure," I tell her, honestly. "I want to take three months off, and then . . ."

"Have you thought about child care?"

I haven't, not yet.

In this brief exchange, I realize how our perspectives already have begun to separate, and how dramatically.

What for me continues to be a wash of experience, of dream images and possibility—each day so new that I have barely grasped hold of it before it is over—is to a woman who has never felt the swelling of life inside her own body a more rational, linear process. First you do this, then you decide that, then you arrange the other.

I know too that at the heart of Linda's questions is one that she doesn't articulate. Motherhood versus a mature creative life. How am I going to keep my creative self, my writing life, alive once I am a mother?

Though it would have assuaged her, for some reason I don't tell her about the writing I did at Menemsha. It is still too new and raw, still germinating and in need of a sheltering quiet. Living creatively, living in full engagement, requires learning to trust the process, be it an orderly garden, a poem, a child.

*

IT IS GOOD to be home. I can't describe the joy of arriving last night at dusk, pushing back the heaps of cold, matted leaves and finding slips of green. The sedum is gorgeous at half an inch, a glow of green crowns. Even the mint by the steps hides a few fresh leaves.

This morning, I step onto the stone path. I need the garden. But I know that the garden alone isn't enough. I intend to inspect the snowdrops and grape hyacinths beginning to poke up along the back fence. But instead, I find myself balanced on my now quite rounded hips in front of the garage.

Its green doors, old wooden things on rusty hinges, were the first eccentricity that spoke to me about the property when we considered buying it. I've resisted several attempts to replace them with even the crudest of mechanical conveniences. The truth is, they'd be more fitting on a horse carriage. But I love them, and so they stay.

I work at the stubborn latch until it opens. A jumble of tools, bikes, ski equipment, and who knows what all greets me. The air is rank from cut grass and gear oil. It smells like my grandfather's workbench. It smells like a farm.

All of a sudden, in the back wall just above the garden beds, I see a picture window. I see a desk bathed in southern light, shaded by a shelf of flowering plants.

A room in the garden.

A place to contain, to pattern, to stitch and write. Such a room would be a shelter for all of me.

I return to the kitchen and begin to draw up plans.

When Mark comes home, I am ready.

"What would you think about my taking over the garage?"

He pours himself a glass of wine and stares into the bottom of it.

"Where will we put the mice?" he asks at last.

"I'm serious," I answer.

My office upstairs is the only feasible space to put the nursery since his, a glorified closet, is too small and the guest room down the hall is indispensable for out-of-town relations. Even if I *could* create a makeshift work space there, I tell him, it is too close to what would be the nursery for me to work with any concentration.

"I've measured. I can use ten feet square, give or take. That will leave enough for everything that's in there now if it's properly organized. I do need a place to work, after all."

I've also called David, a reasonably priced carpenter who'd done some bookshelves for us. He estimated the job, minus electrical work, would cost in the range of five thousand dollars—for dry wall, a floor, and a bay window. Assuming that I will work part-time for a while, this seemed affordable.

Mark starts making a Caesar salad.

My experience of freestanding rooms has been limited but of unalloyed perfection. Whenever I've had the chance to borrow a friend's cabin, when I spent a month at the MacDowell Colony in Peterborough, New Hampshire, my work far exceeded my expectations of it, in quantity and quality.

How often in life do women have the chance to create a room of their own at the very center of the lives they are actually living? A place to create, to sort through, to integrate their many selves? Until now, living in a man's way in a man's world, I've had nothing to integrate. If I'm going to leap into the adventure of trying to weave a mother's wisdom into a woman's work, I need to plant myself in the thick of it.

I get up and help grate the cheese.

TODAY I CLIMB into the attic to find my copy of *A Room of One's Own*. The cover has been taped at least once. The book is old and gray, underlined beyond recognition. I bring it down and take it into the yard where I can read and watch David and his assistant, a soulful dark young man named Pete, tear out soft struts and rotten sills. The expanding barrenness of the garage space fills me with indescribable pleasure. It is pure and dazzling potential.

I am discovering that it is one thing to read *A Room of One's Own* at nineteen, unpublished and ripe with illusion. It is quite another to read it at forty, pregnant, with a lifetime of writing behind one. When Woolf states, for instance, "The book has somehow to be adapted to the body," she is alluding not just to the creation of books. She is writing about all of women's creative work. What she means is that women ought not settle for the standards and terms of work set down by men. Rather, we need to establish the terms that suit *us* and if we do, we will create works of genuine originality.

What are *my* terms? They are different than I once thought them. They involve the thirst for beauty. For meditative silence. And for at least a part of my workday, they require work that taps into my deepest sense of calling. My terms of good work are essentially terms of relatedness—relationship to the right things and the right *kind* of relationship to them—not of dominance and manipulation, but dialogue, reciprocity, response. Beyond this, my terms include a balance between doing and reflecting, between hard labor and head labor, between work and rest, between giving and replenishment.

I can quite easily envision writing for a period of each day alternately with mothering and gardening. "Part-time," as it is traditionally construed, doesn't accurately reflect what I am describing. I am thinking not of a series of roles, of fragments, but of a whole, composed so that periods of "rest" from the intensity of intellectual work would foster and enlarge upon my creative writing life. I might read to a baby, make a meal, work on a quilt. The effect, ideally, would be a communion of parts that satisfies my many dimensions.

Woolf speculated that not only the *form* of our work, but its *content* will be different from men's. Further, she argues, it ought to be. In claiming the space in which to define our work, women shouldn't aspire to reproduce what has already been produced by men. We should envision new forms based on our own sensibilities. Once women are fully at home with themselves as sovereign and autonomous creatures, she writes, our work might take forms we haven't yet conceived. We might not write novels, plays, histories at all. We might not form corporations or traditional businesses. Or not as we have known them up to now.

"Perhaps," Woolf writes, "the first thing she would find, setting pen to paper, was that there was no common sentence ready for her use . . . [And] there is no reason to think that the form of the epic or of the poetic play suits a woman any more than the sentence suits her . . . No doubt we shall find her knocking that [novel] into shape for herself *when she has the free use of her limbs;* and providing some new vehicle, not necessarily in verse, for the poetry in her . . ."

I return to my office in the house and take out the writing that I did at Menemsha. It is like nothing I have ever written before. It is an assemblage of soul moments, a narrative of a woman's life written from an interior point of view, each as they would have been dreamed at the moment of living them.

I am quite moved by what I have done. It is strange, but it is also beautiful. In it I can see that, at the deepest levels, the mother wisdom, the sister wisdom, never entirely abandoned me. Quite out of reach of my rational self, she had stored up the hidden and far more significant story of my life. I don't know what will happen to these stories, but what matters is that the door has been opened once again.

If women give themselves permission to accept Woolf's challenge, will we not produce new art forms, new social forms, new ways of working, new institutions? Isn't this the direction in which my thoughts began leading me that afternoon at the beach at Menemsha?

Women do not need to accept the inadequate models of work, life, family organization that have been imposed on us. The earliest novels were filled with crazy women who lived in the attic. Maybe this is why over the years I have stored so many of my "hidden" creative efforts up there. I love the idea of taking the crazy women, all of them, down and letting them loose in the room of their own devising.

*

MY ROOM IS ready. Michael was here last week to paint, inside and out. The rug man has been by with his samples. I shocked both of them.

"I assume you want Spanish white," said my painter, who has covered every wall of my house over the years with varying shades of off-white.

"Not at all," I replied. I spread out sample cards of periwinkle and bright yellow.

He looked from them to me and back again.

He frowned. "You're pregnant. You need to remember that. Do

you know what you're going to do about this when your hormones have calmed down? You're going to kill me!"

"I want it to remind me of the ocean," I answered. "I need to feel that I'm by the sea."

"Hmm."

My professional room will, I've decided, be home to seedpods, bird's nests, and shells. To a jar of paintbrushes, to art books, drawing pencils, and lots of good thick paper, a basket for my yarns and a space on the floor for my baby to sit in the sunlight and play.

NINE MONTHS of pregnancy have taught me many things that twenty-odd years of successful employment never did.

They have taught me patience. They have taught me that pain is an inevitable part of growth. They have begun to teach me that there is a life greater than my own self-important existence and that this is something worth sacrificing my own happiness and security for.

I've learned that my true work is both more arduously physical and more profoundly spiritual than I had ever conceived and that the garden, a basket of yarn, a long chat across the farmhouse table with whoever drops in, all are the essential counterparts—the heart and soul—of days spent earning our livelihoods, tussling over computers, reading reviews, debating politics. I see what the color and the care, the sensual and the cerebral, the pen and the trowel, can lead to: a brilliant integration. This is the best way I know to remain receptive to the eros, the fecund heart of life itself.

Mosses rise, jewel green, back by the stones. The garden is lovely in an amateurish way, a little awkward, unbalanced, exuberant. The strawberries have been bearing since May and the bees seem glad of it. The sedum has sprung, like so many nosy roses lording over its space. And lavender, chamomile, lilacs, ferns, and sweet Nancy and woodruff in memory of my days in the country, nearly a year ago now, when life first began to flow back to me.

*

I AM THE MOTHER of a son. I take in this fact over and over again as the two of us wait in one another's arms just outside the delivery room. Day turns to darkness. Time has not yet begun, or has just ended. Or we have never left the oneness of my body.

I remember standing at the hospital window looking down at the street as it was coming to life again. Morning rush hour had begun. From the world of offices and Neiman Marcus suits, I have journeyed to this place that could be the first day in the first garden. And how extraordinarily organic, more dreamed than willed, it has seemed.

I see as I never have before the sensuality of all fertility. Only in the flesh, in our bodies, in our works, is transformation possible. Without the willingness to embody, to be broken open with simplicity and power and heart, all of the ideas in the world, all of the ambition, the power, and the achievement—is utterly meaningless.

MY SON SLEEPS on blankets of near dream, the instincts of the pup and the angel in one, gripping at my bones, my flesh, as if I will save him from each imagined free fall back to where he came from. Then softly drifting, his soul a white kite, he sails behind closed eyelids so far from me that he leaves me speechless in his wake.

Breezes and morning birds. We rock one another to sleep like spent lovers. In the old pine rocker, I sing little songs. They are chants mainly; I am too far gone for melody. I bring in the crows and sparrows, kindred winged things, then the garden's gentle populace of chipmunks and finch. Only song seems to comfort him in the dawn, still his sparrow gape. And if I gaze too long, I choke on words of love and praise.

A vase of greens from the garden sits next to us on the bedside table. Lavender and mint, strawberry blossoms, and a single red rose. I am fighting greedily to preserve the peace of this time between us—a place outside the world, sans phone, sans visitors, sans clocks. He sleeps. A fan brushes the rabbit-brown crown of his hair and I begin to tear up again. I play him Vivaldi; music assuages the sharpest pangs of love. Around his body, I straighten, carving air, cleaner lines, the simplicity that I crave for him. It is the peace of the womb and the garden that I want, and of the monastery.

WHILE THE BABY SLEEPS curled up against my body, my right hand steadying him, my left is feverishly about my work again. I have brought out the writing I began at Menemsha. Pages come flying off the pad, then silence, as I gather my bearings or stop to nurse, then begin to write again.

I seem to have been granted a sort of spiritual and creative reprieve. In what little part of me is able to apply perspective, I am quietly grateful, quietly amazed.

THIS AFTERNOON for the first time, we move ourselves out to the deck. I plant William in his bouncy cradle on the table where we can smell the apples, green and hard on the laden tree next door, and the lavender and mint just below.

I wonder if I might earn a livelihood in such a way that the work flows from a life as rich and whole as mine is now, out of such profusion and flowering?

This is the challenge that I intend to set myself.

My room in the garden sits in dappled afternoon shade, waiting.

$\mathcal{U}nity$

IT IS SIX in the morning and I have dragged myself out of bed for
the only hour of quiet I am likely to get in the next twenty-four. A
month into motherhood, it is clearer than ever that whatever its
joys, the luxury of time of one's own isn't one of them. It's a good
morning when I can finish my coffee, scribble a few notes, then
content myself to watch my son, learning his signature ways
through the many delicate gestures of his miraculous body.

Until now, a certain inexhaustible awe has offset the fatigue of
sleepless nights and swaddled me from the grinding absolutes of the
job. I've learned how to diaper, read fecal hues and nocturnal cries,
how to bathe my child without drowning him. I've kept my equa-
nimity amid the household's squalor. Beneath the tangle of these
never-ending tasks, I know that some new order is forming itself,
some new arrangement of life, and that I need to let it compose
itself out of sight, in the depths of an unhurried silence, before I
tackle it head-on.

I've come to marvel too at the women I am getting to know (like fish in a school, like lemmings, new mothers seem to track one another, find one another in grocery lines and at the park), who can tidily stash the infinite number of objects that so suddenly and stealthily litter every surface of kitchen and bath: nipples, bottle rings, diaper covers, bottles. Or organize their infant's laundry as if they've been doing it all their lives. And I am brought low by the heavy competition, those mothers with diaper bags at the ready, stocked with fresh wipes and a granola bar, a spare plastic bag for soiled gear, and an extra bottle of milk.

But each day, I grow increasingly aware that at its most consequential, the job of being a mother doesn't entail establishing proper nap schedules or changing table routines or even finding the right sitters—though these matter a good deal to both of us. Rather, it is how well I am able to honor and foster this unquenchable, undeniable *person*, my child, *and at the same time* form a life that will take both of us into account in our many and diverse needs.

Insofar as I can "create" at all, how can I make such a life for us? What sheltering environment does the essential self need? What degree of simplicity? What stimulation (and defense) from the outside world? What balance of inner exploration and external experience? In these mornings that always end too quickly, I ask myself what inner resources and as yet untapped wisdom do I need to meet this unfolding, daunting task.

I hear him stirring now in the other room and go to him. His eyes are already trained on the space that I move into, prepared for the whispered greeting of my voice. He smiles, shuts his eyes, waits to be picked up. There is such touching strength in his vulnerable trust that I pause again in amazement. The vitality and intelligence of an infant never cease to affect me. My son compels me to be as intensely focused on my life systems as he already is on his.

As I rock him back and forth next to our bed, I know that I want him to experience the creativity and harmony that come from encounters with beauty. I want him to trust in the adventure of being alive, in his silence and in his relationships. I want him to know joy.

I am keenly aware that helping him to learn these things will require a consistency I've yet to master in my own life. And herein lies the challenge: Consistency seems best accomplished if life is kept simple enough that one is able to tackle its demands with full attention—and furthermore with *intention*. Consistency implies an integrity of parts, a conscious correlation between who one is and what one does, even if the range of one's demands is considerably varied.

We moderns, however, have been conditioned to be hurried and restless and inconsistent. We make no such choices. We lose ourselves many times over in the course of a single day. And there is no one to hold us accountable.

An infant, much to my amazement, does. That is, if we allow him or her to.

The uncompromising absolutes of his life offer a rare opportunity to confront my own, and from out of this to build a life that is worthy of both of us. My practices of silence have helped me to reach through the moments of chaos this month to a steadier place within. But I need to press on, to go further in putting what I am discovering of us into the service of a more coherent whole.

✴

THIS MORNING I leave my two-month-old in the hands of a sitter for the first time and drive to the Vietnamese section of the city. I hadn't planned on working again until he was three months old. But this assignment from *Mademoiselle* seemed a good one and a way to get my feet wet in the world of work again. The world

tumbles in—articles, calls from colleagues, offers of projects—and
to a certain extent, I have welcomed it.

I park in front of a nondescript gray Victorian. A young woman is
waiting for me at the door. Plain and simply dressed, without a
trace of affectation, she greets me. At twenty-four—nearly half my
age—she is a nun. I am here to discover what the life of such a
young woman is like in this materialistic, image-obsessed culture of
which we are both a part.

The first-floor rooms that she leads me through are spare: early
Salvation Army coffee tables, molded chairs designed more for
virtue than for comfort. They remind me of the many diocesan
offices I've entered over the years, either on professional or family
business.

The kitchen, however, is another matter. Potted plants crowd
the windowsills, humorous notes are taped on the door frames, the
refrigerator is a collage of bright Post-its. Sunlight spills across the
jars of colored beans and handsome table mats. We have arrived at
the energy center of this home, full of what I call "hearth energy"—
everything that women seem to express when they are alone, and
safe, together. All of it bespeaks a palpable, joy-filled community.

My mood lifts. We go up to her room, and for the next three
hours, my hostess talks earnestly and unselfconsciously about her
vision of her life, sitting on her bed, a cozy nest of stuffed animals,
devotional icons, and books surrounding her. She is a trained
social worker. Early in her career, she had the acute insight that
her work needed a large amount of prayer and reflection to be
worth anything; it needed an anchoring in a life of the spirit.
Because this seemed so countercultural an idea at the time, she
felt that she needed the support of a community of like-minded
women.

Here, she tells me, she has found what she was looking for. Her
four housemates all work in social-action agencies, in schools,

halfway houses and clinics. They gather for meals, they meditate together, they conduct rituals regularly in the front parlor.

I look across the heap of stuffed animals at this woman. She is a youngster in so many ways. Yet she is so full of an integrity that I am longing to find in myself again. I feel myself envying her her life. Her centeredness. It all seems possible here: the soul making, the creativity, the care giving, the intimacy and a purposeful work in the world. It can be done, and done well. I am humbled into a silence that doesn't often befall me at the end of an interview.

We retrace our steps downstairs. It is time for her to go to work, she tells me. But I am welcome to stay as long as I care to.

Around us the house is silent. The rest of the women are at work. I could be alone for the first time in more than two months. We say goodbye in the chapel, and I listen as the front door closes.

The "chapel" is really a meditation room, filled with artwork the women have produced, or collected, over the years. A fabulous library of poetry, psychology, and feminist theology lines the shelves. Candles, bells, and handwoven fabrics cover the tables and stools.

I sit down on one of the cushions. I think: The silence, the symbols and the rituals performed in this room all support these women in their lives and their work. They provide a daily source of integration—not a "sometimes" affair, dependent on priests or husbands, babysitters or bosses.

I find myself thinking further: Discovering one's integrity is a sacred work. It is perhaps the most sacred work we are called in this life to perform. Can any of us do it intermittently or without the right structures of support or alone?

What about mothers, I wonder? What about normal, everyday women, trying to do the miraculous?

There are so few sanctuaries in the day or in the week that most women can enter alone and set our souls down into the deep. Our time is bound, wrapped to our literal, earthly circumstances like a net in which we are caught. And in the absence of genuine re-creative space, we reach for substitutes, for accomplishments or distractions, to maintain the illusion of a Self. In the urgent trivia of our daily lives, we maintain, and cope, and yearn. We do all of this to a certain extent in a state of spiritual exile. And silently.

WHEN I RETURN HOME, I find it difficult to settle down. Eva plays in the living room with William. I can hear him laughing joyfully. All of this is intended to reassure me, I know. And yet it cuts clean to the quick.

Eva is herself the mother of a two-year-old son. She is a bright young Honduran woman who could easily find work in a bank or a service job. Instead, she chooses to be with other people's children, because she believes that it will make her a better mother when she goes home at the end of the day.

Eva has an ease about her. Like the nun whose house I've just left, she isn't going it alone. Her extended family sees to it that the children are cared for while their parents work. The adults are always finding jobs for one another in times of need. They nurse one another's sick, entertain one another—and through all of the difficulties of cultural marginalization and relative poverty, they manage to celebrate together, often and profusely. Last week, after working a full day, Eva cooked up chili for thirty people.

This afternoon, I regard her with a certain amount of envy as well. In a single day, I've encountered two women who are doing a better job of integrating spirit, heart, and their labors than I am.

I take a cup of tea out to the garden.

What are *my* priorities, my enduring values?

In the first days of motherhood, life and work, soul time and creative time flowed together as I haven't known them to in years.

Ideas and writing came in torrents some days and could be fit into nap times and even feeding times, if the phone didn't ring and there was no one stopping by for a visit. But the moment I rushed into this assignment, impulsively and without reflection, the delicate balance, the internal consistency that I had made was shattered.

I began to compartmentalize. I became a divided self, external to my life. Work became objectified again. So, to a certain extent, have my relationships. But this is the last thing that either I, or my newborn infant, needs.

My son isn't even three months old. Why am I doing this?

If I am to be ruthlessly honest, I have to admit that I am trying to make a point, assert the first principles of my feminism, that a woman's talents oughtn't be suffocated by motherhood. How many women before this have I—with no experience of being a mother myself—applauded for working up to the onset of labor pains or for managing to resume office work the moment they are out of hospital and on "maternity leave"? It is "resistance to the mother" all over again, as we extend workplace orthodoxy to the realm of child rearing, the same norms of efficient productivity and competitive "excellence." How have I been so reckless?

If I am to achieve the unity that I desire, I can't be so vulnerable to my impulses and reactions. Hasn't this time of self-examination been all about cultivating this higher quality of consciousness? Discovering the threads of a simpler, more composed and intentional life?

In the arbitrary (perhaps fear-conditioned) choices of the past few weeks, I haven't been *integrating* anything. I've simply put back into place a piece of the old self, hoping that it will fit because it is now a bit smaller than it once was.

But smaller in relation to what? What vision of the whole informs me and my choices these days?

Just as I am about to go back into the house, the phone in my office rings. It is my editor at the magazine.

"I know that this is delicate," she begins in her impossibly indelicate, toughened voice. "But the art department wants to know — have you found any *pretty* nuns?"

I replace the receiver and stare out the window in what Virginia Woolf calls an "annulled" mind: blank, overextended, cluttered. I am as dry as the blown peony buds of June, brown and tattered on their bent, overextended necks.

There must be another way, a more organic and morally sound relation between a woman's Self and her work.

Much in the garden has become incidental since the baby's birth, untamed. The euonymus and nightshade run amuck around lilacs. Suckers shoot from the roots of the crabs. Much has come in on winds and whims and settled in with no more fashion than a fruitcake. Every year before now, I dutifully weeded out the ajuga and sorrel, clipped back the ivy. Not long ago there was a scheme, a pattern, a discernible form. A row of crabs and alternating lilacs ran the length of the border. Rocky woodland plants thrived in orderly fashion farther back, and an English shade garden lay hushed along the periphery. Now all of it is in a state of desuetude.

I need to study the old wood, in my life and in my yard, to see what will remain, what can be strengthened, and what needs to be removed.

Next year, the garden says. There will always be next year. But there will never be a first year of life ever again . . .

*

I'VE CANCELED Eva for the day. I make a strong cup of decaf, wrap the baby in his snuggly, and carry him out to my room in the garden.

As I arrange a blanket for him on the floor, the fact isn't lost on me that in spite of all the care that I took in designing this space so that he could be at home in it, today is the first time I have brought him here.

I prop him on his side and we regard each other under the shadows of the sheltering trees. All is golden and rust outdoors, and this brilliance, splashed onto the white woodwork, elevates my spirits and gives me hope that I *can* recapture the promise of this room.

It is delicious to be together. We nuzzle and play with each other's fingers, touch skin to skin, roll a terry-cloth block and hear our answering laughter.

For the first time in my life, I understand how the quest for stability and predictability leads women to return to their professional lives as soon as possible after the birth of a child or a wrenching illness or depression. Though they may feel ambivalent about doing so, the challenge of finding new forms of balance is just too overwhelming.

For the first time too, I understand the women who decide to stay home with their young children, to withdraw from the consuming demands of conventional career advancement while trying to attend to the equally demanding life of their families. They sacrifice a good deal in the process, for they must accept the excruciating burdens of living in a society that, despite its lip service to families, remains largely indifferent to their needs.

This is a white-knuckled time for women, when the choices we make—whether about motherhood and career, power, sexuality, sacrifice—seem the only possible ones. Most of us opt for the tried-and-true. The challenge of attempting to create more original, customized work arrangements is too lonely, and the struggle to envision the way life *ought* to be too painful, to endure in isolation. We huddle with our kind, women who've made similar choices, as around small and threatened fires, our backs to the dark shapes and the voids beyond.

But none of the choices are entirely satisfying. All of them seem to be boxes from which it is difficult to escape, much less to clearly see the sky. There is the choice of the status quo ... there is the rejection of the status quo. There is the part-time compromise. We turn from lives of assertion and ambition to lives of simplicity, but in doing so, we too often relinquish relevance and larger purpose. We fail to evolve from our individual solutions a more public and broadly applicable vision of life that might be whole and balanced for all women.

It is hard not to conclude that we have not yet finished a true "revolution." We are living partial lives, lives that don't nearly resemble what we might wish for ourselves, lives that don't take us at our best or use our wisdom and various energies as they might best be used. We lead lives that force us to accept intolerable compromise and we allow far more of our fundamental integrity to be chipped away than we should.

Things *should* be different.

Before the derailments of these past few weeks, I felt as if I was moving in the right direction. Perhaps my error was in wanting to believe that I could have it both ways, the old and the new, stability and change, security and experimentation.

Maybe my starting point must be to realize that one cannot change and yet be the person one was. The transformed self must accept a certain discontinuity with its own past.

What was good and worthy of the old life—my writing, my significant loves and memories—needs to be re-envisioned in a new context. If, as I have wanted to believe, the small changes I've made up to now have moved me toward a more authentic Self, I need to listen to this Self now as it sifts true value from false. Petty ego needs from the truer core that longs to express ideas of real value. The fearful, driven, conforming self from the Self of silence who honors originality. The useful drone from the crazy lady in the attic. At the thought of her, I smile. In this way, with a bit of humor, there is a fighting chance that the old will lead to the better. I will be able to fit a woman's legitimate call to work into what I believe is our God-given command to be whole.

I have set the stage. I have assembled many of the pieces. Now I need to bring them together into some kind of practical daily life.

Weary as William, I settle into reverie on the blanket. I see myself eleven months ago overlooking the sun-kissed blue of Me nemsha harbor, wondering what it would mean to be a mother. I remember thinking long and hard about how women must learn to better mother ourselves. Like any newborn thing, our lives in transition are as fragile and in need of protection as the children, or the new dreams, that rouse us regularly from sleep. I look at my journal, so full of dreams. I take in all of the colors and the objects that I have gathered in this cherished room. It will take more than dreams to make us whole. We will need to go through hard labor.

*

I AM STANDING at the Cuisinart pureeing a batch of apples. I slice another, a MacIntosh from the farm on the other side of the hill. Its cross section is beautiful, crisp, and greeny-white, and wonderfully sharp of scent. It is what an apple is meant to be.

At its center, in the innermost furl of its vital life, dance the seeds. Were I to cut it crosswise rather than down the middle, I would see this quality much more clearly, for thus arrayed the seeds make a star or a mandala—symbols of possibility and wholeness in one. Around them, the flesh holds the mark of maturity, the fiber that embodies the apple's raison d'être, its purpose in becoming. Finally, there is its skin, the container that maintains and modulates the environment for the whole fruit.

If only my days, seen in cross section, could embody the same variation of elements. If only my days were as organic and felt as ordained!

Just as I finish the last of them, Eva arrives for the morning, and I head out to my office.

I've begun trying to put my ideas about a good, organic life into practice. For a number of hours each week now, I gather short stories about contemporary motherhood to put together as a collection. It is stimulating work and certainly relevant, but its chief advantage is that it doesn't require travel or arduous professional pyrotechnics. Most important, it enables me to be bolder in the new creative work which I realize matters most to me.

I've pulled out the stories that I wrote at Menemsha; also the notes I've made in the past year about all that I have experienced as lost in me as I pursued success in a culture that trims women to fit its needs.

I have begun to write in a new way about these topics. I am trying hard to hew to a riskier and higher standard of truth telling, and to allow my "first thoughts" to find uncensored expression. I am no longer trying to find answers that fit into familiar forms. Rather I want to place the questions themselves before the universe with new faithfulness to my own truth.

I bring in my observations during the course of my days as I am now living them, my thoughts between sleeping and waking, my concerns about the necessary balance between physical and intellectual nourishment, between solitude and companionship. I bring in memories: my old beloved barns and my beans, Marianne Brock and the shells of so many ocean walks. I probe everything that seems to matter for what it has to teach me about the way women need to live to claim our wholeness.

Rereading my journal has been invaluable. Culling the bits of insight and truth sprinkled in among the many passages of worry and self-doubt becomes a means of affirming that inner authority which I am trying to make more "life worthy." When women find ourselves in a cultural reality in which wholeness, balance, harmony, and rightness of living are no longer part of a visible or viable reality, we need to seek their images where they *have* appeared, in the wisdom of our own pasts and in the past of the culture. Through them, we may begin to discover what arrangements of work and family life can make lives for us that are creative, coherent, lived from the center.

The very effort of winnowing my own fragments of written or dreamed truth is encouraging me to sense that the feminist "revolution" may have stages that we're just beginning to explore; or, better, that the individual story of modern womanhood can have a happy ending—perhaps not as a story at all, but as a poem, an essay, or new forms such as Virginia Woolf hopefully predicted in *A Room of One's Own*. I am beginning to love these few hours when my door is closed, the phone is turned off, and the breeze from the garden filters in through the window.

SOON THE MORNING COMES to an end, and the intense physicality of motherhood resumes. It is a welcome break. For so many years, I believed that the rhythms of domestic life were fruitless—literally, mindless. Now I am astonished at just how beneficial are the rhythms and variations between mental and menial, solitary and companioned works, how they instruct and delight.

When I am cooking, music playing in the room with me, or when I arrange lavender in a vase by the window, often I hear through the music, or see in the variable brilliance of sun swimming through cobalt, just the image that I have wanted to complete the poem on my desk. As I sift through journals for memorable moments from the past, I have become so much more attuned to the humble sources of meaning that are all around us, in the life just beyond our front doors.

I eat a bit of cheese and grainy bread, stuff an apple into the sack that we will take on our walk, then we set out up the hill for an afternoon stroll. Over and over again, I am aware of seeing life for the first time in years, and this intimacy with my surroundings invites a far richer connection than I once felt from dashing out of the office for a quick lunch or coffee break.

Life is no longer divided between "my work" and the neutral surround that either supports or frustrates it. I want to find others who are similarly on the journey, weaving for themselves and one another worlds of greater wholeness. Who is trying to organize people in worthwhile local projects? Where might I find them, so that as woman and son we might join them and further our adventure of being alive together?

Sometimes we stop to read a notice, follow a lead. Reading hours, exercise classes, worship services, a weaving class—all of these and more catch my eye. There are as many ways into the experience of connection as there are individuals on earth.

Finally, we return home, where the day's meanderings can be gathered while we rest before the dinner hour.

THE KITCHEN COUNTERS ARE crowded with color and life. A bowl of peppers and peaches brightens the farmhouse table, lemons line the windowsill, and cookbooks are always lying open. The cross section of the apple might provide me a useful metaphor for the variability of my days. But its quality, its history and provenance, give me food for thought and action. Where did it come from? What was sprayed on it while it was developing, what poured on its leaves in the way of fertilizers? When was it picked and how was it ripened? I've never been as interested in food as I am now that I am responsible for feeding my son with nutrients other than those from my own body. He is too young to chew, but already he loves avocados, peaches, apricots, and shows a distinct preference for fruits and vegetables.

The more I think and read about such questions, as about the questions of community life that I have carried in the door with me, the less trivial the domestic and the "nonprofessional" become, the more political and moral my attention to their many aspects.

And so, another work comes into being. I decide to spend part of my mornings now investigating reliable food sources. Considering whether I can adapt part of the garden to cultivating my own food and learning how to preserve the seasonal organic produce that I can obtain locally. Finally, I begin to chop vegetables.

Soon enough, once again, the house is quiet. The day's gardening is finished and all the stories told. A few quick notes in my journal, a bit of light reading, perhaps a few stitches worked on a sweater, and it is time to return to the deep waters of sleep, until I am washed up once more on the unknown shore of another day.

I've known poetry and the joy of the body, I've formed physical order, matter, and beauty, "weaving" a pattern, touching all dimensions of the being that is life itself: seed and fruit, flower and stalk, flesh and skin. If a woman were to touch down on all of these dimensions in an average day, couldn't she be said to be living a whole life?

The balance would shift and vary, of course. Something in us is always coming to life, something else reaching completion. But at the center of this amazing cycle would stand the wholly realized Self, watching, entering into, becoming.

It is this Self that waits for us, when we have sifted out all the false, the identities born of projections, fantasies, fears, from our genuine potential as women. To rediscover what is authentically ours, we must ask:

Where do I feel most alive? What works are truly legitimate and worthy of my commitment? How, realistically, can I distribute my physical resources among the many demands on me? When and how must I take the time to be still and pray?

There is no particular orthodoxy, no formula, to this. Each woman must find the appropriate shape for her own life. But I believe it requires us to begin by accepting our *own* terms of creative response, rhythm, and balance. To get to know these deeply and well, and to learn to act—and when not to act—from them. This is the great leap of love.

When we do all this, I believe that we will become the women we were called to be. And then, we will begin to create new works and new ways of working. My insights as a mother might become the basis for my engagement with larger social issues. My respect for intuition and the spiritual life might become the basis for a new kind of outreach altogether. When one lives, or tries to live, in a condition of wholeness, then the call to devise a "work" that embodies the same principles of balance—between ego and transcendence, between the personal and the public, between mind and heart—becomes, it seems to me, inevitable.

Now that I have watched my son for endless hours, I will never again doubt that humans, like plants, are born with innate, distinctly individual intelligence. I have watched his hands dance in what I now recognize as his characteristic wave patterns, his voice pitched just so. They are gestures entirely superfluous to any demand for food or dry diapers, warmth or contact. They are gratuitous, necessary, and beautiful. In them, as in nothing else, I find myself observing the singularity we call personality, mind, and soul.

At midlife, I draw on far more than a set of sweet, inexplicable gestures, but the lesson is the same—a gift from the universe for my taking. If I give this mystery the Self the appropriate space and light, affirmation and nourishment, it will assume its true shape for a new season.

TWO

A New Life

Women desire *worlds*—places of inner and outer freedom in which new forms of connection can take place . . .

In other words, women struggling against the constraints of conventional feminine modes of relationship desire *not less* but *more* (and different) relations; *not disconnection, but connection that counts.*

—CATHERINE KELLER,
From a Broken Web

Sabbath is a way of being in time where we remember who we are, remember what we know, and taste the gifts of spirit and eternity.

—WAYNE MULLER,
Sabbath

Change can be lonely.

Loneliness can be disabling. It can cause us to question the truth of our inner realities, our feelings, and undermine our capacity to act from their authority.

The first step is the journey into the Self.

The second, not far behind, is the journey in good company. Only in the company of fellow seekers can our dreams become reality. Women need to transform our dreams into new lives, into new ways of being, new ways of relating, a new culture. From our dreams—written down, painted, sung, shared, and acted upon—we will begin to create places where the life-affirming presence of the feminine can live embodied in the world.

Finding right relationship is the most important single step a woman takes in trying to transform her dreams into reality. It is the first step toward the new, as she finds her way out of essential solitude into the world again.

How will I find such companions?

THE FOUND ELEMENTS

Reality

1

ONCE SPRING BEGINS to draw the snowdrops out of slumber, I'm restless to venture out. I wrap the baby in his hand-knit blanket and on a balmy April morning set his stroller toward the center of town.

After what feels like a lifetime of days curled in front of a fire with cardboard picture books, the town's brocade of stories lures me like a shot of espresso. The vegetable stalls and the African American bookstore are doing a thriving business, the nail salons, the yoga center, and the check-cashing services. Vicariously, I feel held here, where grandmothers raise the children while the adults see to business, where laundry lines cross and you can smell soup cooking as you walk to an evening meeting with the sister-in-law next door while the men play dominoes or watch baseball. I feel a warmth, a gentleness, that I never experience in the middle-class professional offices where I used to return to file my stories.

Maybe that's why I left them. It is a good lesson to have learned, that I prefer the atmosphere of places that retain the presence of grandmothers and their threads, binding their children into a collective shawl of meaning.

I cut into a cozy neighborhood that I know only by reputation. A warren of botanists, gardeners, artists, and social activists, it has produced more than its share of the town's innovations and quirky traditions.

Some of the homes are ramshackle, some spruce. In between are a motley of greening plants and used cars, partly finished sculptures, tire swings, crude tree houses, dogs, and overturned tricycles. I come to the end, a sprawling green swath—part community gardens, part public space beside the subway line. Beyond this stretches the more congested low-income neighborhood of apartments and row houses occupied by large Latino clans.

I am just about to retrace my steps, when to my right, I spy a large and curious looking whitewashed structure. It isn't a home. It is too big and architecturally odd to be a home.

In this part of town, it could be anything. A New Age commune. A pagan cult temple. A Buddhist shrine. A crude sign hangs on the door. It reads: SPONTANEOUS CELEBRATIONS. Inside, the lights are on.

Nothing ventured, nothing gained, I think, as I step out of the sunlight and in through the door.

I find myself in an enormous dim oak-paneled work space. It is filled with large tables covered with half-finished projects involving construction paper, paints, brushes, fabrics, and many bottles of glue. A preschool, perhaps, I think. Or an artists' studio.

Now I can hear someone in a kitchen down a corridor to my right, stirring what is unmistakably a pot of curry. Whoever it is doesn't seem the slightest bit disturbed by my presence, for the sound of the spoon doesn't hesitate a stroke out of concern for my worthiness.

I feel like a child in a fairy tale who's happened into a furnished cottage, complete with soup and bread, after days of wandering in the forest.

There is a gentleness here, a restful peace that seems to exude from the walls themselves. I feel the urge to linger, but I still have no idea where I am, or whether I should be here.

I'm about to leave, when I see a staircase. I decide to follow it. Perhaps there is someone on the second floor who can help me.

I come out in the middle of a large room in which a woman, seated serenely and entirely alone, works on a piece of green fabric. When she hears my footstep, she looks up and smiles. She is in her early fifties, I guess, with graying blond hair and brilliant blue eyes.

"Are you here to help with the costumes?"

Only when she says this do I notice the massive paper trees and stilts, veils, and murals, propped behind her against a full-sized stage.

Then, seeing my bewilderment, she laughs.

"I'm sorry. We're doing a production of *The Magic Forest* tonight," she explains. "It's wonderful, full of woodland creatures and forest gods. I'm Femke," she stands, extending her hand, her eyes twinkling.

I find my voice at last. "What do you do here?"

"Lots of things," she says. "Basically, we try to build community through the arts, helping people honor their traditions and create new ones. We do a lot of festivals. Not long from now we'll run the 'Wake Up the Earth.'"

I had heard of "Wake Up the Earth." It was the neighborhood's major spring event, a daylong affair that started with a parade of giant puppets and costumed children and spilled into the community gardens across the way where people partied until dusk.

"How long have you been doing this?" I ask.

She invites me to pull up a folding chair, happy for the company while she works.

"We've been in this building only a year," she answers. "But we've been doing what we do for more than twenty."

"When we moved to town, I was just beginning my own family," she goes on. "I was an art teacher. At the time, there was a lot of negativity in the neighborhood. White people were moving out. People of color were moving in. A lot of people felt that the neighborhood was deteriorating."

Though I didn't live here at the time, I lived not far away, and I remember this as a grim no-man's-land of shuttered storefronts and street gangs. Even after the neighborhood began to show signs of improvement, with new shops and restaurants moving in, many outsiders were afraid to visit, much less to move here.

"A group of us began looking for alternatives," Femke continues as she stitches. "I think that having young children is a time when people are more open to creating change." She looks up. "You want the best for your kids. You pay attention to nutrition and to creating a better world. I wanted to start an alternative school for my children—in this very building—but I couldn't find anyone to help me buy it.

"At the same time, there were all these women moving in from distant places who had this incredible need to do their culture and give it to their kids, to keep a link with their roots."

Femke happens to live just around the corner from this building, she tells me. Day after day, she'd walk her children down to the rubble heap of an abandoned playground on what is now the community garden land, desperate to find solutions.

Finally, she decided to open her own home. She made a stage in her attic. She ran a summer arts program out of her basement. While the children played, the neighborhood's mothers would make up the next day's projects: puzzles, sewing activities, handmade presents, and costumes for the regular dramatic events held in the attic.

Soon their efforts extended into the underprovisioned local schools. Femke and her group of mothers brought arts-and-crafts supplies into the classroom. They directed local art projects. Before long, they were staging public festivals at the spring and fall equinoxes. The festivals and the art projects became so popular, and began to involve so many local people, that the city started to provide them with modest funding. Through it all, Femke continued to raise her four children. She conscripted them into the festivals and projects. She took time to be involved in their schools and to throw herself into several local redevelopment standoffs with the city. She helped start a food co-op, and when the real estate prices in the surrounding streets began to soar, she refused to sell out and move to a cushier part of town.

Now her children are grown. But it is inconceivable that she would quit working with the community, she says. She has drawn women from an amazingly diverse range of backgrounds, all of them devoted to using creativity to develop vital relationships in the random environment of an urban neighborhood.

Women of all ages gather here, she tells me. Some work full- or part-time elsewhere during the day; others are at home raising young children. In the afternoons, the building is used for an ongoing Latina quilt project. A group of Dominican women use it as a meeting space for their world-peace projects.

Femke puts down her work and looks me in the eye. "We're really an underground network of women," she says. From a small-scale summer neighborhood program for their own children, this network has created a potent institution that brings together the many elements of the community's quilt, old-timers and ethnic newcomers, young and old, stay-at-home parents and working professionals.

With their long-held dream of having their own building now realized, the group has a greatly expanded vision of what they are about.

"We want to create an environment where people can join one another in expressing their creativity," Femke says. "A place where parents will come with their kids, where we celebrate our different cultures in a rich, stimulating environment."

On Monday and Friday evenings, people from the neighborhood can drop by for macrobiotic meals and music by local performers. Classes in yoga and art are offered during the day. And with a certain poetic justice, last fall two young women approached Femke with the idea of starting a community-based preschool where we are sitting.

Femke gently smiles. "I felt like I was seeing myself twenty years ago."

Femke used to leave the neighborhood and travel several miles each day to work. She could be earning a big salary in an affluent public school system, I think as I study her. Instead, she has used her professional skills in the service of a vision that grew from her concerns as a mother and a neighbor. She had the courage to put her vision out there, and thanks to instinct and persistence, found women of similar mind who seemed to have been just waiting for someone like her to come along and give a shape to their longings. Together for some twenty years now, they have succeeded in leading lives that model admirably the message of creativity, engagement, and balance that they have tried to impart. They work together, play together, and smooth the way for one another's niggling daily responsibilities, the child care and the "must-dos," in order that their other important work "in the world" can become reality.

When the doors open for the performance of *The Magic Forest* tonight, the craftsmen and computer professionals, housekeepers and restaurant workers from the surrounding streets will bring their children into a well-lit place where women are determined to see people whole and offer a sanctuary for that wholeness through creativity and homegrown culture.

"It's a window of opportunity," Femke tells me as I thank her and prepare to leave. "If you can gather those forces, you can do wonders."

✻

ON MY WAY home, I think about Femke's phrase: an underground network of women.

Have I, in the course of my many journalistic encounters, met other women whose life circumstance and inner need have similarly converged to create lives that are more integrated than mine has been? Can I summon to mind women who have made their personal challenges the seeds of new works and new ways of working?

What might such extraordinary lives teach the rest of us, whose job descriptions may be more routine, whose dreams are less dramatic, whose apparent choices are more limited? Are there lessons in such stories of transformation that might benefit those of us who are searching for a path from fragmentation to wholeness?

BACK IN MY OFFICE, I open my files and comb through them, pulling out articles, skimming old interviews.

One of the first that I encounter is Katie Portis. At first blush, Katie hardly seems a likely candidate. Katie was a streetwise heroin addict who'd mothered several children.

Yet hers is a story with the same hidden thread as Femke's, and the same courage as well. It is the tale of a woman who struggled successfully to pull the fragments of a self—mother, worker, community member—together into a new life as a community leader.

Katie once told me that to survive as an addict you need to be as wily as a Fortune 500 executive, and as I came to know her, I believed her. For years, she managed to pull off a madcap scramble between using and earning or grabbing what she needed to buy her drugs. Somehow she found a way to maintain her habit and keep her children fed and herself out of prison. It was a perverse balancing act that often required her to be in two places at once, two people at once.

But one day, the various personae collided and fell apart, and Katie discovered firsthand the terror of a mother's forced separation from her children.

That day, Katie decided to come clean. And the moment she did, the fragments united and new purpose was born. She knew that, whatever her work once she got free of her dependency, she wanted to have her children with her. She wanted to use her own experience to change the lives of other poor, desperate women in her community, to show them that there were better ways to live, if they could come to believe in themselves.

Her own bitter experience had taught her that a woman's children are her strongest—and in many cases her only—incentive to live drug-free lives. She determined to found an all-natural detox house for women. Her detox facility would be the nation's first to allow women to stay with their children during the traumatic process of healing.

Support and like-minded people seemed to materialize from out of nowhere. A new life was begun.

When I met her, Katie was living, breathing, and sleeping the process of detoxification with every woman who came through her door. She acted as guardian angel, as nurse, sometimes as militant mother superior, and as a model of change. Her detox house, Women, Inc., was located in the same neighborhood where she had once used drugs, serving thousands of addicted women as a safe place where they could be nurtured back to health and to a new life of their own.

Katie's message to them was this: Survival doesn't have to entail fragmented and self-destructive lives. When a woman takes *her* reality in hand, survival can be a thing of strength, hope, and generosity to oneself and to others.

CLEM BARFIELD, the next file I come to, learned this lesson in the hardest way a woman possibly can.

Clem didn't seek change. It was what she did with change when it came to her that makes hers an extraordinary story.

Clem was a veteran of Detroit's planning department, when her son was shot to death by a fellow high-school student in a meaningless skirmish. Up until then, Clem had played by the feminist orthodoxy that said: Work is one place, home another. The rules that said "real" adult women tend to "adult" matters and leave their children in the hands of others. Rules that unintentionally but tacitly had leached authority from black community elders and handed it over to the children and their ineffectual overseers, the teachers and the police.

With the death of her son, Clem declared war on the rules. Her only resource was a mother's grief. She called a gathering at her church one night and invited other families who had lost children to street violence. A hundred people showed up, most of them mothers. They wept and prayed. They agreed to create a support group right there in the neighborhood where their children were killing each other. She quit her downtown job and started a community safe house and called it SoSad (Save Our Sons and Daughters).

Clem used personal tragedy to create a life that was more expressive of her values, and a work that tried to make these values a reality for those around her. Her vision was to change the status quo.

By the time I met her, she and SoSad had earned a city-wide identity. The second floor of a renovated schoolhouse out of which she worked in one of Detroit's roughest neighborhoods was a busy, involved kind of place that had a feel of genuine sanctuary and hope about it. Children and young people came and went. The phone rang incessantly. Clem would interrupt our conversation to reach for it, and I heard her voice saying over and over again, "I'm sorry. I'm so sorry," with the incontrovertible authority that seemed a balm to those in crisis at the other end. She staffed a twenty-four-hour grief hotline. She went to the homes of families whose children had been killed. She helped them work with officials and make funeral arrangements. She referred them to grief professionals.

She invited families who'd been victims of violence to speak at public meetings downtown. Clem and her group staged rallies and appeared en masse, a visible presence for authorities and children alike to see. They had one message, one dream. They wanted the violence to end.

Over ten years, Clem's war on the rules changed those rules. Detroit's violent incidents had dramatically decreased and its children were safer. And most of this was due to the mother who took her convictions to heart and made them a reality in the neighborhood where her own life, and loss, was grounded.

I CLOSE MY FILES and step into the garden.

Middle-class women aren't exposed to the same pressures as poor women. We are protected, and to a certain extent protect ourselves, from them. But that only makes these stories of transformation and integration more impressive. For all women are struggling with the same internal pressures, the stress of too many priorities, insufficient time, lack of emotional support, and the absence of restorative quiet time. It is no longer just a segment of women who need help in learning how to live healthier, saner lives. All of us want the pieces to connect for more than a few serendipitous seconds each day. Whether we drive a Saab or take the bus, live in an apartment in Queens or in a suburban home in Fairfax, Virginia, most of us long for lives that elude us.

These stories challenge me today in a way that they didn't when I first wrote them. They set off new responses, now that I have come to consider the possibility that women's realities, our ways of seeing the world, and our solutions to the needs of others and ourselves may very well be different from men's—and now that I've begun to suspect that our ultimate integrity and happiness depend on our reclaiming these differences as our own contribution to the culture.

I want to learn from women whose visions have achieved a satisfying, womanly rapport between the public and the private parts of themselves, between mind and soul, spirit and creativity.

I hear my journalist's voice speak up for the first time in many months, saying: Go in search of these women today. Find out who they are, what they believe, and what they have to teach you.

2

OVER THE COURSE of the next few weeks, in the grocery-store line, on the playground, browsing the flood of publications that come through my door, I begin to hear and read about women who *are* creating new realities out of their own transformed visions.

I HEAR ABOUT a lawyer in Portland, Oregon, who left her legal work after some fifteen years of tenure to run a Montessori school and spend more time with her own creative projects.

I HEAR ABOUT a law partner, a graduate of Radcliffe College and Harvard Law School, who left her firm and its sixty-hour-a-week demands to tutor public-school children in Cambridge, Massachusetts.

I REMEMBER the book editor who left the corporate track to set up a literary agency in her garage at home so that she could see her children after school and, equally important, sell only the books she believes in without the pressure to make a killing in the literary marketplace of useless blockbusters.

I READ ABOUT a Chinese-born immigrant, a woman without children of her own, who got a group of unoccupied Philadelphia children to help her turn inner-city rubble into a sculpture garden. The garden was so successful as a rallying point for neighborhood improvement that today, known as the Village of Arts & Humanities, it offers free classes in art, drama, cooking, and gardening, and its twenty-five employees build affordable housing on its periphery.

AT LUNCH WITH a friend, I meet a woman who spent years working and traveling to Africa on behalf of UNICEF. Several years ago, she left her job and founded a local ecology newspaper, produced by inner-city high-school students. The paper aims to educate minority youth about environmental matters and simultaneously to encourage literacy among at-risk populations. Each month now, instead of her junkets to Mozambique, she ventures into largely black and Latino neighborhoods close to her home to work with young staffs in putting out another issue.

I am becoming increasingly fascinated by the many faces of this "underground." I start a file and place it where I can see it every day on my desk.

Every day, it seems to grow.

＊

ONE DAY I find myself at lunch in a neighborhood vegetarian restaurant with a woman I've just met. Ann Moritz is in her late forties, alert, with a ravishing mane of red hair that offsets her wonderful green vest and batik skirt. At forty, she left the perfect corporate job for a more balanced and socially relevant life.

As she munches on a tofu sandwich, she describes the job she loved as the newsroom personnel director for *The Boston Globe*. A Kansas-born girl with a zeal for racial justice, for seven years she reveled in the freedom she had to recruit talented minority reporters. She traveled to hiring fairs around the country, networked relentlessly, and usually ended up getting who and what she wanted. For a long time, just knowing that she was filling the newsroom with new voices, and new perspectives, on the city's notoriously difficult race relations, was fulfillment enough.

"But," she pauses, "the longer I stayed in that position, the more I realized that if I *really* cared about the issue, I needed to be operating on a broader scale. I needed to be immersing myself in what was happening in Boston in general, and not just in the publishing industry."

Other realities had entered the picture for her as well. When she was thirty-six, her second child was born, and she and her husband moved from a cosmopolitan urban neighborhood to a bedroom community just outside the city.

It troubled her that she left her children each day in a fairly homogenous white, middle-class world for the "higher ground" of racial engagement miles away. Not only did her work life prevent Ann from enjoying the geographic flexibility to expose her children to a larger world, it also boxed out the time she might have used to be involved in her community's life on her terms.

"I also felt like I was outgrowing what was there," she says of the job.

Ann began to weigh her options.

"I spent three years thinking about it and about a year talking to people about it," she says.

She considered going part-time. She considered getting herself hired by a consulting company that specialized in diversity issues.

"I wanted to hold on to my career," she tells me. "And I didn't see any businesses that I wanted to join. The ones who were working in this area were doing it in far too formulaic a way for me to be interested."

She attended several motivational seminars to prepare herself for life "outside" the corporation. Finally, at forty, she struck out.

She set up a room on the second floor of her home and began calling on her old sources—only now as potential clients. While her children were in school, she began moving in corporate circles throughout the region, meeting with clients and teams of collaborators, professionals of color from all walks of life whom she had met over the years and who now form her closest relationships apart from her family. Together, they try to change the racial face of Boston's corporate leadership.

The difference, now, is that her work has become squarely planted in the terrain of her daily life, near her family and her neighborhood, giving her the opportunity to integrate them all.

Within a few years of starting her business, Ann took on the job of managing her town's multicultural festival. The festival had traditionally drawn on the smattering of diverse populations within the community and abutting city neighborhoods for a day of interactive crafts exhibits and mingling.

Ann approached an African American musician in town. Together they hatched a fairly radical scheme for the predominantly white town. They would launch a gospel choir. Today, the Milton Gospel Choir performs at about twenty functions a year — in addition to the festival, where it has become the main event.

People in town tell Ann that it has changed their lives. They feel part of something that is culturally and personally meaningful. They get together socially; they work together to recruit new members. They even make quilts together.

Her new life, in turn, has changed Ann. Changed her understanding of relationships and her sense of what is possible.

"It has taught me more about working across class lines and culture than I had to do in the workplace," she tells me. "It's sharpened my awareness of the shortcomings of dealing with groups *that are based in the workplace,* rather than in the place where people actually live. People live and are active in a place because their hearts brought them there. So teamwork becomes a process, not a professional task. If you find a way to bring out the best in everybody, there is a lot you can accomplish. It's a true model of sustainability."

Family life has changed in Ann's home since she decided to change the rules for herself. Last year, her husband, previously a single-minded professional, decided to run for a post in the neighborhood association. This past year he also ran for, and won, a seat at Town Meeting.

"He was out from 7:30 until 11:00 last night," she says laughing, "and he wasn't bored!"

Her children, as they have grown, have become more involved in race and cultural affairs. One is sixteen, the other fourteen. These days, her son is a drummer for the choir.

When she isn't working or singing, Ann now has time to be involved in her children's schools, where she has chaired the diversity committee.

"I'm either part of the solution or I'm part of the problem," she says. "I'm not comfortable if I'm not advancing things somehow. I have the same attitude toward my work, with my town, and with my kids' schools. The least I can do is go in with a constructive sense of how I can help change the environment.

"It's vital to me that I model an ethic of giving back and that my children understand in a real way our link to a common humanity. I'd be happy going to my grave doing what I'm doing now," she says.

After we have said our goodbyes, I return home. There is a message waiting for me on my machine. It is from Ann.

When I get her on the line, she says, "I just wanted to ask, how many women of color are you including who are changing the rules?"

I tell her about Femke's many groups of immigrant women, of Katie Portis, about the Chinese woman, Lily Yeh.

It hits me then, the real force of this very real underground.

Unlike our earlier feminist "movement," which helped white middle-class women break into male professional enclaves, this one is truly inclusive. It crosses all lines of womanhood: race, class, and age. It embraces married women and single, working-class mothers, suburbanites and city women.

All of them are saying: There is something more. There is an alternate women's reality in which significant work, significant relationships, and significant creativity are possible, all at the same time. Some of these women work full-time and more; others, part-time. What distinguishes them from women who've opted for the tried-and-true isn't the number of hours they work outside the home. Rather, it is that in changing their lives, they dug deep to discover their *own* creative response to the realities around and within them. They allowed their concerns as women and mothers to determine the content of their work—and its rhythms as well. Their lives as mothers, professionals, and community members form organic, inspiring wholes.

These stories and their inclusivity are about the most hopeful thing to have come along in American culture in a very long time. I thank Ann for her call. She's allowed me to see just how inspiring it is.

3

TODAY IS a day at home. The baby sorts Cheerios close to my feet, singing little songs like a crow in a field of alfalfa. Domestic activities provide the lull I need for welcome reflection. I've been surprised, simply by opening the most ordinary of doors, at how many women are successfully changing the rules, constructing lives around *their* passions and needs, not someone else's. I want to consider more closely the steps that they've taken to get where they are today.

I start to pull together the makings for a soup stock, salt and peppercorns, rosemary and thyme. Occasionally, I have tried to skimp on my stock, finding the vegetable drawer less than profuse with carrots, or the bag of celery irremediably limp. Or I haven't given it the four hours it really needs to reach the proper complexity of texture and taste. The results are invariably thin, my time feels wasted, and I end up sacrificing the batch to sauces—as accompaniment, not the foundation for a meal.

This time, I'm giving myself both resources and time. Fresh carrots, peppers, and peas from the farm stand, bay leaves and garlic and chicken from the organic market, and a whole day to simmer and set before it is put up, a portion for today and one for the future.

I turn on the classical radio station and set to work.

As I scrape the carrots and watch their ribbons fly off into the sink, I try to identify what set these women on their divergent life courses.

In every case, it seems, a combination of outer and inner forces, welcome and not, worked in tandem. A career disappointment, a sudden death, a bottoming out or a "leveling out," the arrival of children—all these changes in circumstance demanded a more creative response than they'd had to give their lives up until then. What is different about these women than most is that they *allowed* themselves to acknowledge the unacceptability of life as they were living it. From somewhere deep inside, they had to summon great stores of honesty and a willingness for self-examination and risk.

To a woman, I believe they would say that they'd come to a point where they wanted their work to have greater relevance—to society and to their own immediate lives. Acknowledging their own fragmentation seems to have opened their eyes to the segmentations and injustices in the world around them. They wanted to be able to respond to both inner and external conditions with greater attentiveness, compassion, and energy. They wanted to work alongside others in genuinely connected ways, not in provisional relationships, to be available for school visits and field trips, to achieve a better balance between work, personal relationships, material-consumption patterns, and community life. Finally, each woman, in time, realized that she wanted greater opportunity for self-expression.

I stick cloves into the onion, fill the pot with water, and toss in the vegetables. Then I begin to play with the spicing. Each time I make a stock, it is slightly different. Today, I throw in a pinch of nutmeg.

The challenge for each of these women was to imagine a new shape for their lives and find a way to make it reality. For Clem, the answer rose with lightning speed. For Ann and Elisabeth, the

woman who founded the environmental newspaper, the process
was more gradual. A period of gestation began. The surface of
life remained unaltered, but in the depths, they entered a process
of questioning and self-reflection. Old habits of mind, earlier
expectations of success, had to be let go, replaced by some newer
value.

Interestingly, I suddenly realize, none of these women mentioned finances as a primary concern. This wasn't, surely, because
finances weren't important. They were. Several of them support
their families alone. But it was as if the changes they needed to
make had become so important to them in an intellectual, moral,
and emotional sense, that they'd made a conscious choice not to let
fear and financial anxiety interfere.

Each expressed a willingness to accept responsibility for the
financial consequences of their choices. At the same time, each
exhibited a confidence that, as heretofore successful women, they
would find a way to make the changes work. Quality of life had
become more important than the latest Ferragamo shoes.

And in the end, each one of them did make it work financially —
in some cases more successfully than in their earlier corporate lives.
They thought. They talked to others. They sought advice and
know-how from professionals, neighbors, friends.

They listened to themselves. They spent time with their journals. They thought some more.

This went on, for most of them, from a year to three years, from
the first inklings of change to the first steps in the directions of a
new life.

And change, when it did come, was gradual.

Though Femke wanted her own building from the start, she
settled for using her attic and basement.

Clem started with a modest church meeting, a handful of sym-
pathizers, and the interested support of the local media.

Katie began with sobriety and the compelling nature of her own story.

Ann got her foothold one client at a time, relying on her savings to carry her through the first touch-and-go year.

There were the other, less obvious steps that each of them had to take on their journeys from dream to reality. There were the growing pains in trying to knit together pre-existing life patterns with new sensibilities and newly recognized energies. There were the days of trying to fit a nine-to-five output into the hours that one was used to putting into a leisurely morning staff meeting and answering one's e-mail. There was learning that you can't read poetry while your children are having soccer practice, where neighbors gather to bond and swap tales from school. There was learning that you can't say yes to an extra work project if you plan to meet with your women's group, attend a church meeting, or talk to your neighbors at the same time. All of these hard new, uncharted ways demanded discrimination and the patience of a mule.

Persistence was essential. The truth is that we learn by living into our priorities. We can only think so long and so hard about how to put the ingredients together. Then we have to live it, in order to discover the right variation for us.

I have learned from my own year of making soup, gardening, and venturing into making sweaters and quilts again that each undertaking has its own best form, evolved over generations of trial and error. This is true of poetry, music, a satisfying piece of prose. In each case, "the best" seems to involve that which most successfully integrates a complexity of elements, whether spices, metaphors, or chords. We know when we have heard a great poem or tasted a superb salad—we do not need to be told.

Women today are still struggling with our form, the optimal balance of needs, desires, responsibilities, instinct and consciousness, sensitivity and ambition that make us whole. Too many of us have allowed our workplace, with its paternalistic patterns, its hierarchies and definitions of success, to dictate this for us.

These women are different. They are daring to say that their *life* in all its diversity, not just one part of it, *is* the form. They are willing to risk their own variations on what it is to be whole.

I've decided to make soup today because the work spaces of these women felt like kitchens to me, or hearths. They didn't literally contain pots and cookie jars—not all of them, at any rate. But they were threaded through with a kitchen's alchemy, with the presence of children and dogs and garden tools and mealtimes.

The steady rhythms of solitary application alternate in them with the creative rhythms introduced by children and neighbors. And all of these elements mingle in becoming nourishment for body, mind, and soul. As in the best kind of kitchens, these lives defend the value of the small and the intimate, of closeness and interdependence. Creativity becomes one with public giving. Beauty and culture are rooted in the here and now.

There is something else at the center of these lives, around which it seems to me the varying balances, the warmth and homey informality and natural hospitality flow. This is a silence and a certainty—a sense of timelessness. It is as if the works these women are employed in (quite humble and mundane works, taken singly) reach beyond the present, into the more eternal work of human history.

For these women, existence isn't about "having it all." It is about "being all," being real in all of their many and varied dimensions. They see life as a process. They know that priorities will shift and that change, growth, and transformation undergird any life that is truly alive. These are beautiful lives: harmonious, internally balanced, comely.

The soup has been simmering for two hours and smells divine. I skim off a spoonful, let it cool, and taste it. It has been a long time since I've made such a good batch.

Though I can't quite imagine inviting the neighborhood in for a weekly potluck, or tuning up the piano for a sing-along, or lighting a bonfire among my hyacinths to celebrate May Day, Femke and these other women have lit a fire under me.

I go out to my garden room and look through all the stories that I have collected in the past few months. Perhaps theirs, along with my own, will be the makings of a new work.

Ritual

BOLTS OF AMISH RED, blue, and green cotton swamp the length of the dining-room table. Two weeks ago on a trip to the library, I found myself detouring into the adult art-book section again. I wanted the books on Amish quilts and Navaho weaving. I envisioned them lying open around the house, inspiring me at odd hours of the day.

I am being drawn to images again. It is as if I need them to awaken something in me, as if I need to step outside the world of words to gain access to the deeper, less polished and less articulate core. Silence, with guiding eminences.

I found what I wanted and checked them out, then headed directly for the fabric store. *Making* something, I decided, constructing my own images in a pocket of the day when I was able to find silence, might do the trick.

In one brief impulsive hour, I'd embarked on a crib quilt for my brother's new son.

Now, once I put the baby to sleep, I come down to my glorious disorder of fabrics and threads. I pull up a chair, cut and sketch and read. My husband comes home to find me poring over the animal motifs of northwest Native American women, or the Hand of Friendship templates of the Quaker women of Pennsylvania.

I really have no idea why I am doing this.

I haven't a clue what it is that moves me so about these traditional forms, or what I am looking for in them that isn't satisfied by the other ample opportunities for creativity that exist in my life. The last thing I need is another project.

One day in early October, my friend Peyton comes over for tea. While we are waiting for the water to boil, she wanders into the dining room. One look at my table and she wheels around and comes to lean in the doorway.

"You need to come with me to my workshop," she announces.

Peyton does "definite" very well. A Wellesley graduate, she spent years in the financial world. When her second son was born four years ago, she left to pursue her first passion, which is painting.

I look into her direct, not infrequently urgent, brown eyes. Their expression is rendered even more urgent this afternoon by her freshly blunt cut, ruler-straight brown hair.

"What would I do?" I ask with a dismissive shrug.

"You just need to come," she repeats in her firmest voice.

The next week I find myself in a narrow side street in the industrial outskirts of Cambridge. The rents are cheap and studio space plentiful here. At a dead end, following Peyton's instructions, I park next to a set of train tracks. She is there waiting, and this time she is smiling.

"Come on," she says. Then after a pause, "Are you ready?"

I shrug.

"You're going to love it."

She leads me across a blacktop toward what I consider a fairly questionable exterior staircase, attached to an equally questionable-looking warehouse. I can't imagine that it has been touched with an eye to maintenance since the leather industry died here seventy-five years ago.

I can't help noticing, though, that the base of the building has been planted with a riot of brilliant nasturtium. I've brought with me some threads and a needlepoint canvas. But the minute we survive the teetering staircase and emerge on the threshold of a large, bright studio space, I see that my planned project is far too timid and much too constrained a foil for what I am, admittedly with trepidation, about to experience.

A primitive cavelike structure made from silver foil hangs from the ceiling pipes. Affixed to it are clothespins and spools woven with colored wires to resemble human beings. The effect is totemistic, as riveting as any of the primitive animal imagery in the books that lie on my dining room table back home.

Peyton gestures to a loom farther on. It is made out of twigs, laced with scraps of felt and feathers. On the floor near it sits a rune of river rocks and flat black stones. Partially completed canvases are tacked on the walls. I notice a potter's wheel in the corner. But most of the creative activity that goes on here seems to draw on the recycled cones, plastic rods, children's play beads, kitchen beans, yarn, cloth, driftwood, and seashells that are housed in bins and shelves that line the length of the opposite wall. It is work that tends to the ritualistic, clearly; work that approaches—I can't quite believe that I am using the word—the sacred.

The women who have arrived before us are already established on the floor or on stools. They work with a gentle but focused intensity that invites no interruption, no small talk. Peyton and I seem typical. We are all roughly middle-aged, educated, and serious.

In the middle of this calm intensity, an older woman sits on a braided rug pushing a pile of pinto beans into a spiral shape on the floor. Peyton brings me before her.

"This is Kate," she announces.

Kate is the studio's founder. I learn that she has been doing this work, refining and evolving it, for going on twenty years. With a nimble dancer's body fit into loose purple overalls, she looks me over, smiles broadly, and says simply, "Welcome! Just dig in."

I look around. Peyton has already laid out her series of bright pastel nudes of pregnant women and has launched in. I've mentally dispensed with my needlework, so I approach the bins of materials. As I do so, I find myself fighting waves of self-consciousness that carry me all the way back to my six-year-old self on the first day of school—wanting so much to look like I know just what I am doing, when in fact I haven't the slightest idea where to begin.

This is just one afternoon out of my life, I tell my guilt-ridden, task-oriented self. I'm only here on Peyton's behalf. Life will go on when I leave. I can go back to my nephew's quilt when this is over.

I find myself sidling into my comfort zone, over to the cupboard of traditional gear with which I am familiar: paint and pastels, ink and clay.

I gather a handful of pastels. Quite obviously, this isn't Studio Art 101. A deeper, more interior kind of self-expression is taking place here. It will be enough for one day, I decide, not to be overly ambitious. I will simply reacquaint myself with some of the good old things.

I choose a place on the floor in the middle of the activity and soon am happily rubbing the colors onto paper, getting my fingers thick with blue and yellow dust. I transfer the process of layering and rubbing to the unbleached needlepoint canvas I've brought with me. Using long strokes of green, then blue, a bit of terra-cotta,

I manage to create a lovely, if not terribly useful, ground of deep cobalt and spring green.

Menemsha colors, I recognize suddenly. Pond colors.

I haven't the faintest idea what I am up to. But after a moment, none of this matters. I am completely absorbed, and taken in by, the process. I feel indescribably free.

Kate leaves me to myself, for which I am grateful. From time to time, she stops and asks questions of the others; gentle, probing questions. It seems from my novice's vantage point that the image is key here; the image is that which each woman is working to discover.

Kate probes, challenges, then backs off and leaves them to work again on their own.

I am just about to take a break and eat the apple I brought for a snack, when one of the women, a beautiful, frail-looking brunette, sinks to the floor in front of her work and begins to cry. Without missing a beat, Kate goes over to her. She lights a small candle beside her, then sits quietly until the woman has composed herself and is ready to go on.

I am deeply moved by this gesture. It is at once so intimate and so respectful, so knowing. I get up and go over to the library of art books that line a small alcove, and curl up in a nest of pillows. I try to bring some perspective to my own morning's work. What would Kate make of my Menemsha associations? What do I make of them?

I feel as if I've wandered about as far from the orderly world of the old quilt makers as I possibly can. I have stumbled onto a path. One that leads me to a storeroom of images, a place of remembrance and love that is deeper than words, as personally solid and strangely satisfying as the templates of those old stitchers. This is a place that I haven't gone, except for my few brief experiences in

solitude, in a very long time. It is like dropping a plumb line into
the soul.

Peyton joins me.

"Well," she asks, "how are you doing?"

I don't know how to answer. I am not sure that I understand half
of what has happened.

I want to understand.

I know that I will come back.

A WEEK LATER I return, this time empty-handed. I greet the
same women and a few others, some of whom have traveled great
distances to be in this obscure corner of Cambridge, Massachusetts, pushing beans and meditating over brush marks they've made
on pieces of white paper.

As we gather the things that we want to handle for the day, we talk
quietly about our lives since we last were together. I am somewhat
surprised to discover that most of the women don't think of themselves as artists at all. They work in mainstream jobs. One is a therapist. Two hold midlevel administrative positions in local companies.
One works for a university. The older women have raised their children and have more time on their hands. They are able to attend art
shows up and down the east coast, and they bring their exhibition
catalogs and reactions with them to the group when they return.

I share little about myself. I am so aware of being in the midst of
change, of redefinition, that I don't want to identify myself with an
occupation that no longer feels entirely right to me. What little I
can share is the common strand: Clearly all of us are seeking a way
back to a more authentic relationship to the Self through the
images that we travel here to make.

We move about, mixing paints or sketching, arranging beads on
cloth, or pieces of driftwood into makeshift shelters. When we are

ready, we retreat in silence to the spaces we've chosen for ourselves. There is a ritual quality to our preparatory movements and our work, and this ritual quality, which extends through the afternoon, feels deeply right.

As the day proceeds, we remain gently aware of one another's presence. We get up to replenish our materials. We break for a snack or a cup of tea, return to sit with our backs against the wall and study what we have done. We write in our journals. Sometimes people change tacks entirely, to work on poems, paint, or draw. At the end of the morning, we gather. One by one, we share what we have done. Together, we explore the images that have surfaced in the "work" of our deep play.

I think about the women I have recently met in my community who have changed the shape of their work and their lives according to their own bold re-envisionings. Those women offer me lessons in objective *results*, public and visible change. Here, I find, I am beginning to experience the counterpoint to such inspiring end points, in a "way" to authentic change. The images that arise from the depths claim a value in me, or elicit an unexpected but decisive symbol of what wants to come alive in me.

After years of therapy, encounter groups, solitary reading, and various support groups, I feel as if I have come home. This workshop of women feels like ground zero, a place of acceptance and, what is more, profound understanding and insight about the ways of the soul. What we do here on Tuesday mornings week in and week out isn't just a way to achieve change, but a way to continually nourish the deep sources within us.

ONE WOMAN HAS BEGUN to interest me a great deal. An older woman, she tends to work very quietly off by herself.

Each week she gathers the same materials—beach glass, stones, a few shells. She kneels and arranges them on top of a piece of colored cloth, as if she is praying. Intensely self-contained, she at the same time conveys an intensely open, receptive quality as she pours herself into the image that gradually emerges under her hands. One feels that one way or another she has been about this work for a long time, and that each beautiful mandala she creates is an efflorescence of a much deeper and continuous current of thought and reflection.

During a break, I learn that she spent many years as a painter before beginning to work in these evanescent mandalas.

"There have been times in the last two years when I too have been tempted to give up my earlier work altogether," I tell her. "To stop writing, adopt a code of silence, and make some work of my hands—gardening, quilting—the employment of my middle years." I pause. "I try to imagine where such a life would take me, what new understandings would cut through the blanket of words in which I've swathed myself."

She listens and nods. She tells me that this kind of exploration is essential. By midlife, we usually need to go into those places inside that have fallen mute as the other parts have taken over, with all the trappings of the ego in the world.

"Often by then we no longer know whether our work is serving the community's real needs, or if it even reflects a worthwhile ethic," she says. "This uncertainty in itself creates a limbo of the spirit and deprives our work of its meaning."

Hollowed thus, our work can't fulfill our real spiritual needs. To compensate, we become compulsive. We work more and more, and increasingly automatically. We seek power, material reward, ego gratification, for what we sacrificed (or what was sacrificed for us) of the deeper spiritual satisfactions of work that makes us whole. And much as we may try to rearrange the external elements of life—a new job, even a new way of working—we need first to go

down into our center, to find there the insights from which we
need to act.

BACK HOME, I return to the books on my dining-room table. As I
turn the pages, I think how remarkable it is that certain motifs and
practices pass from generation to generation intact in communities
bound by common tradition. This must be because they continue
to express basic truths about the community's relation to ultimate
meaning. Those who work with such symbols and materials were
and are often women. Even when they stitched the humble blankets
or threw the pots for daily use, these women had a vital role to play,
for they were doing more than just producing goods. They were
carrying on the wisdom of the tribe. As they wove, stitched, and cut
motifs into objects of daily use, they were calling down the powers
that transform the mundane—task or tool—into things imbued
with the life of the spirit.

Maybe I haven't needed another project as much as I've needed
my work to be threaded through with this sense of its sacredness, its
participation in some ultimate meaning. Lacking a culturally cohe-
sive language of symbols, perhaps all women must find our own
way to the sacred in our work, individually.

THE NEXT TIME I see her, my new friend Lynn has brought
with her a book about the village women of India. These women
rise each morning at daybreak. They slip out to their courtyards
with small bowls of water, rice powder, and cow dung. First, they
sprinkle the ground with the water. Then, with practiced strokes,
they mark out the coordinates of the mandala that they will
spend the next half hour developing into a work of stunning
intricacy.

As they go about this task, the younger girls imitate their elders, learning and memorizing the whorled patterns of tradition in anticipation of the day when, as female householders in their own right, they will lead the morning prayer ritual and impress their own distinguishing flourishes on the earth of their humble courtyard.

The purpose of this ritual is to call down the household deities, to honor and pray to them, that they might guard the household through the work of its day. Mostly, these deities are goddesses, and the mandalas made to their honor become the matrix against which every other gesture of the day will find its hope and its meaning.

At nearby shrines—at the foot of trees or in open doorways—the elderly women of the house kneel. They light incense and whisper prayers. None of the women are excluded from this hour that marks the countryside of India new each day as sacred ground. Using the simplest of means—their fingers, dung, water, and the occasional basket of flowers or dab of handmade pigment—the women accomplish their most essential task, which is to inscribe an arc of consciousness intended to keep them, their families, their labors, and their possessions in its attending wisdom until darkness and sleep guide them to the following dawn.

Against the inevitable exhaustions—the daily labor alongside the men in the fields, feeding and clothing their families, caring for sick children, the ill, and the elderly, even the knowledge that their handiwork, their ritual art, will vanish in a matter of hours, trod under by human and animal feet—these women prevail. Why? Why do they continue to perform these rituals, day after day, year in and year out, generation after generation?

Because it is their true and necessary work. Without it, nothing else would have meaning. It is the work that binds up all that is secondary, transitive, merely human, and gives it larger purposes, in and beyond time. This is their good work.

The workshop is the place where *we* do this same sort of work. It is where we search for the sacred with the same hunger to be its bearers. Here I don't feel crazy or desperate or shrill. I feel sane, reverent of life and the imagination. I am blessed with the wisdom of women older than I, who have been on the journey far longer than I. Here, in a sense, is church for me. These women uphold a holiness, a wholeness, that I want to stitch into my daily life.

I stop arranging my stones and go sit against a nearby pillar with my sketchbook. Last week, I spent several hours drawing details from Kate's books on Romanesque and Gothic cloisters, in particular, reliefs I found on the capitals of the pillars. Now I open my sketchbook, and all at once, against the foreground of the drawings, I can see that the unfinished mandala I have been working on this morning is a crude representation of a monastery.

Why a monastery?

It is true that whenever I've traveled I've found my way far from the beaten track, to the tops of out-of-the-way mountains and the monasteries hidden there. I've sought out the small ruins of country chapels. I've spent the day. I've vowed to return. I've never tried to justify this attraction—it is just something that I do. I've always found at these places a profound peace and the sense that, even when it least feels like it, there is some larger plan at work in my life, that I am in some way accompanied. All of a sudden, I remember that two of my most significant dreams this year have been set in monasteries.

What have I—a lapsed Catholic and a relatively secular journalist, in a society with a virtually nonexistent monastic tradition—sought with such assiduousness and consistency in secluded places of deep and undisturbed prayer?

Why now, when I am simply trying to play with beautiful natural materials that I hope might illuminate the work that I am meant to do in the world, should the image of a monastery reappear? What do prayer, silence, and solitude have to do with my work?

THE NEXT WEEKEND, I get in the car and head west. I take the
turnpike past Worcester, turn onto several secondary highways, and
am soon driving past farmland on rural roads, headed for the only
monastery I know of within a hundred miles of home. I've been
here once before. It was a frigid January day when we stopped to
buy jam on our way to an antiques shop in nearby Groton.

Today, I want to confront this, whatever it is—image, dream,
longing—in the concrete. In the Now of my life.

I pull into the grounds of St. Joseph's monastery, drive up the hill
past the gatehouse, and park in the visitor's lot reserved for re-
treatants and the few day-trippers like me who just happen by.

The stone chapel is perched at the summit of the monastery's
highest hill. As I walk to the visitor's door, I look out across the
rolling meadow and orchards to the land to the west that I loved so
much and explored so deeply as a young student with my friend
Linda.

I feel a catch in my throat, an unexpected and long-buried emotion. Below me an older monk wanders among the trees. Out of
some inexplicable sense of modesty, or of self-protection perhaps, I
quickly turn and go inside.

The area of the transept reserved for visitors is nearly pitch-dark.
I feel my way into a pew and kneel down. From this vantage point,
all that is visible of the chapel itself is the altar, a beautiful piece of
solid field stone, above which hangs a massive crucifix. This afternoon, I find the crucifix oddly menacing, overbearing, too jarringly
insistent. But the frame of mind with which I've entered is stronger
than the feelings of resistance that now sweep over me, and I give
myself over to an emotion that I don't fully understand. It is part
grief and part relief; it is years deep.

I don't know how long I kneel in this way, my forehead pressed

against the stone wall in front of me. But when I sit back, I am left
with a feeling of astonishing clarity. I open my eyes.

It is a provisional clarity, to be sure. I haven't received any insight
into "life solutions." I don't feel as if I am being called *out* of the life
I have been living and handed a new career plan. Rather, some vital
bond, long attenuated, has just been asserted, reforged, between
myself and my life. I recognize that I am being called *into* it in a
more profound way than I have allowed myself to experience in all
of my years as a "grown" woman.

I hear the monks gather for vespers and I step back outside.

Have I just met God out here on this bleak and beautiful hillside? Have I met myself? Or is it all of a package? The solitude, the
recollected self, the austere and exquisite enclosure of stones, the
presence of a known and once-loved tradition, a world of familiar
symbols?

I remember my dream of the woman in her cloister, surrounded
by her beautiful embroideries and quilts, her shells, her poems. It
was the dream that started this whole journey. Now I find myself
thinking of all the women I know who are seeking a sense of relevance much like this, yearning for reconnection to their centers. It
isn't just the mothers or artists of my acquaintance. I think about an
old college professor of political science who recently told me that
she gets up at five to read the Daily Office of the Benedictine
Order. I know an administrator of an international human rights
organization who attends a weekly women's group at her syna-
gogue. An editorial writer who takes meditation retreats, a therapist
who has become an oblate.

Our small daily "retreats," our meditations, keeping a dream
journal or participating in a workshop, are the modern-day places
where we allow ourselves to hear the promptings of the soul. We
have in common an intense devotion to prayer and ritual. Most of
us have been privately prayerful for years and only in middle age

are coming to see the need for a more serious commitment to our inner lives.

I don't need to join a monastery, but today I have learned that I do need to bring the woman of symbols and of silence more fully alive in the cloister of my heart. I need to make traditional sabbath ways—of refuge, renewal, and offerings—daily ways.

ON THE DRIVE HOME, I pass a small neighborhood church just as a half dozen old women, mostly widows, are emerging from afternoon Mass. Surely, I think, most rituals are mechanical some days. The women of rural India awaken tired some mornings, at odds with the men in their lives, or with themselves. The widows who tramp into church before their second cup of coffee doubtless fall a little unconscious at the unbending recitation of the creed.

But our rituals are the vessels that sustain our true homes in the world. They are the chamber from which the self in its essential silence stands at the threshold to the timeless. Beauty fades. Affect. Strength. The expressive energies atrophy. We burn, rather, within, where all of our strength, if we'd but know it, is and has always been.

I consider the "womanly" works of the past—all the knitting and cooking, the ironing, the tending of gardens and babies that have consumed women's energies for generations. And I see now how clearly and directly women have used them not just to continue the material culture around them with grace and beauty, as communal Sabbath rituals in their own right, but for their own silent purposes as well.

Standing by the stove or seated with a pair of needles in her hands, a woman created the space and the physical rhythms that slowed her down and drew her into her center. In lives that were busy from dawn until dusk, these were brilliant strategies for stitching a bit of the Sabbath into every day, gathering the disparate pieces of the day into a lesson, a point of reflection, an offering of praise, however humble. Such practices were a way of life, a Sabbath life. They were the structures for keeping the soul's orders.

I think of Marianne Brock who at midlife made a practice of poems, of sacred speech.

How do I live a Sabbath life? How will I affirm the soul's orders when I return to Boston and the life with my son and my husband, my work and garden?

The next time I see her, I put the question to Peyton.

"Every day," she says, "I make one sketch. It doesn't matter how crazy the morning has gone or what else I have to do during the day. It doesn't even matter if I have to take Billy to the dentist's. I make one sketch."

This is her ritual.

It is a matter of laying in one thread at a time, working the pattern. It is bringing the ordinary to the quiet, insistent desire of the spirit. The work of one's day becomes whole, a source of affirmation, not a drain on some otherwise frustrated, unrealized personal quest. Our Sabbath ways restore us, feed our souls, renew in us the sense of larger purpose that our lives are serving, and bring us back to the mundane with new energy and commitment.

Maybe I will begin a quilting practice after all. Maybe at long last, I will write poems.

I look at Peyton's huge magenta and cobalt and electric green madonnas with their protruding bellies.

"Next year," she muses, "I think I'll do owls."

For the first time in my life, I understand. Through no conscious intention or design, I have found my way to women who've been known to me and been available to me as friends, colleagues, teachers, but who remained invisible as guides until I was able to ask the right questions. I feel this fellowship rising up now to hold and support me with powerful hands, having realized that their lives, however worthy, wouldn't be complete without a willingness to serve the symbolic life of the soul and the life of the spirit wherever it is to be found, in a day's good works.

Purpose

IT IS STILL DARK above the trees when I rise and light a candle and try and settle myself in the same undivided calm as the flame while I wait for morning's first bird song. Life pulls with its many demands, but for the moment nothing compels me. I am filled with peace; receptive, rather than driven. If today were to be the last one of my life, I would be doing exactly what I am doing now, beginning the day in quiet awareness, grateful that after a long season of wandering—in roles that were only partly right, on paths laid down with only partial self-knowledge—I have come home to my life and its unfolding purposes.

To all surface appearances, it would seem as if nothing has changed very radically about my life. I still go to my office each morning at nine. I still dash to the library at odd hours of the night and reach for my notebook when I ought to be watching the traffic.

But running beneath the obvious currents of life, the writerly habits, and the innumerable symptoms of being a working mother, everything has changed.

The work that I want to do now is different from the work I have done in the past. Around the solitary act of writing has grown a web of commitments that I regard as indispensable "works"—a spiritual life and friendships to be fostered, manual work both solitary and domestic that anchors me in the actual flow of my days, the self-sacrifice by which each day I shed a bit more of what gets in the way of seeing clearly what needs to be done.

I have learned that I need ways to keep me in touch with the "other," wiser, voice within me. I need silence and the experience of beauty, be it a walk in the garden, a few minutes with a treasured poem, my son's sleeping face. When I have these, I feel a sense of harmony that enables me to approach my disparate responsibilities, duties, and creative opportunities alike, with the flexibility and openness of a dancer.

The day I accepted the discontent, the listlessness, and fragmentation that my life was producing in me as real, I began a new life. I knew that existence was more than all these, that I was more than a résumé of public achievements.

If it was power that I wanted, I realized that it was a very different kind of power than I'd ever known before. I wanted power over my own life.

If it was success, it was success not on the world's terms but on my own—and I needed to learn what this meant.

I listened intensely and I looked closely. Amid the continual commotion of daily life, I felt my way—in my morning meditation, in my journal, as I yanked weeds out of the garden or sat at my desk or moved through the days at home with my young son.

I asked myself continually: What is it important to be, what needs refurbishing, what sloughed off? When a piece of the path appeared straight and clear before me, I tried to follow it toward whatever wanted to reveal itself next.

Becoming the person that I have become has been a work in itself. *Being* her, on a daily basis, is an ongoing challenge. I continue to turn to the hours such as this one, that at various times of the day for nearly three years have marked the inner course along which I have come home. If I could take this experience and share it with other women, I would say that it is a journey, a road open to anyone who hears the call to change, even if she has no idea what a changed life will look like. The truth is, none of us do until we arrive. But this only underscores, to my mind, the necessity and the soul-making power of the journey itself. And though the end point is impossible to know at the outset, the stages of the way are fairly clear. With the benefit of hindsight, I see them as three phases that occasionally overlapped and sometimes repeated themselves, but that are nonetheless distinct.

Getting on the Road

IN ANCIENT TIMES, men and women responding to a sense of unease with their lives had many ways of trying to hear God's will for them. They became pilgrims. In relative poverty and usually on foot, alone among strangers, they set out on journeys that lasted days and sometimes months, until they arrived at the holy place of their destination. Here they stopped and stayed for a while, to be still within themselves and to pray.

Both the going forth and the arrival were understood to be sacred dimensions of the pilgrimage, and so too was the return, for the wisdom that the pilgrims received was often encoded, in paradox, in curious dream images. These required the entire trip home (and often more—years, whole lifetimes) to decipher.

I have been reading about this highly respected spiritual tradition with great interest. For, in our own way, we modern women have to become like pilgrims.

Most of us can't entirely abandon worldly life, nor would we wish to. Though we don't leave home in a literal sense, however, we can become more inward. We can shift the emphasis of our time. We can detach ourselves from the nonessentials, from club and association memberships and from needless errands. I shed layers of social obligation, in exchange for silence. We can go out to lunch less often so that we might spend a midday hour in meditation, or go back into the house a bit earlier to prepare a dinner for close friends.

If possible, we ought to reduce our work to the bare essentials, and that which is consistent with our core sense of purpose, for the duration of the pilgrimage. In the diminished "lifestyle" that results from such a choice, we can make do with last year's clothes, drink water instead of wine, make rather than buy gifts—and all of this will only make us freer and happier. I knew that what I was seeking I wouldn't find in the world as I had known it. I needed to travel lightly, to take only the bare essentials and a few well-chosen steps each day.

Finding Companions

"SEEK AND YOU SHALL FIND; knock and the door shall be opened." I had never forgotten these words, recited into memory in childhood. Now I discovered that they were true. Once I'd made the commitment to my life, something in the universe moved. A space opened within me. Not a road to Chartres or to Mecca, perhaps, but a space nonetheless. Some days, it was an hour of quiet, a precious gift of time. On others, it was a glint of insight, a helpful conversation, a recommended book when I least expected it.

The pilgrims of old were accompanied on their journeys by a spiritual leader, often an abbot. At the beginning and the end of each day, he would give shape and meaning to the journey by reading sacred texts, leading his band of travelers in prayer, and teaching the pilgrims how to interpret the day's events.

Modern women have no such guides. Early on, I realized that even a determined detachment from life's diversions and a curbing of unhealthy or distracting relationships weren't enough. Women on the journey need to find ways both to protect the process of self-discovery from the usual noise of daily life and to understand what the soundings of the self are telling us.

The practice of keeping a journal has proved invaluable to me, for I soon discovered that I wasn't alone. My fears, my vulnerabilities, my unresolved wounds, and defenses, my younger selves, dreams, former life visions which had somehow gotten lost in the thicket of the many "shoulds" I imposed (or allowed to be imposed) on me, were my first, and most unexpected, companions.

These will come for all of us, one way or the other, and it is useful to remember in the darker moments that they *should*. Reading about pilgrimages of old, remembering the colorful characters in Chaucer's *Canterbury Tales*, I now understand far more clearly than I did in the beginning the meaning of this journeying with often not-very-welcome strangers.

The strangers in our lives enable us to encounter the lost dimensions of our Selves. Day after day as I lived with my own, we grew more compassionate toward one another, more familiar and forgiving. It was my "strangers" who eventually broke through to the true Self that had lain buried beneath the accumulated roles and habits and expectations I had amassed over the years. I discovered a lost authority, a Self that began to speak to me about new ways of living, of relating to others, about projects and desires that as a mature woman I knew I had the power to realize.

For a long time, the journal was my sole confidante. But I knew that I couldn't change my life by my own will, or even by my limited personal knowledge. We need guides to help us stay the journey and to grow with it. We need to seek out those writers and thinkers who expand our insights and treat them like the close friends that they, in fact, become. I began to read the spiritual journals of Thomas Merton, Teresa of Avila, Thich Nhat Hanh, and many others, as well as books about personal change. In this way, my circle of "guides" widened and opened up new vistas of what was possible.

Keeping Out of the Way

ARRIVING AT the holy place often required a circuitous, indirect route and physical disciplines that weren't part of a pilgrim's life back home. Pilgrims often walked *around* rather than through the large, teeming cities on the way to their destinations, choosing to keep themselves out of the way of old habits and temptations. They were tolerated and even welcomed in the small towns they passed through, regarded as the Everymen of the divine journey. Villagers often provided them with food and shelter. Good pilgrims were wise enough not to interfere with the daily tasks of their hosts. And the truly wise ones returned the hospitality they'd been shown by performing a few chores before moving on.

I believe that some physical practice is vital for women on the journey of change. One that I undertook during the time of my own journey has been gardening. Gardening has grounded the questions for me. It has kept me, literally, down to earth. Almost any physical work, intentionally undertaken, would do the same I suspect. Working with one's hands for an hour a day, whether it is in the soil, with bread dough, with wood or cloth, invites one into the world as nothing of a mental nature really ever does.

In caring for life that is separate from our own, life that depends on us, we are able to regularly place our own drama in a larger perspective. We learn that all good work is subject to cycles, rhythms of evolution, growth, and decay, and that to work well, one must learn to weather such changes, within and around one. In tending my flowers and herbs, I learned invaluable lessons about our vital interdependence with nature. I learned the value of humble routines in sustaining this interdependence that, when heeded, is the best model I know for our human relationships.

If a physical practice like gardening anchors us, it also taps a level of psychic life that many of us haven't experienced for years. Physical work reawakens a delight in the sensual world, in the creative—its colors, movements, and makings. For a woman, these creative impulses are sources of deep spiritual nourishment. I think that I never could have arrived at the point I am at today had I not allowed myself to be led into the physical pleasure of daily life: caring for the garden, making simple meals from its produce and gifts and clothing from my yarns, learning again the body's own language and needs for quiet and care.

I'm a spiritual enough person today to believe that the old form of my life needed to break open and die before the new could emerge. This is what a pilgrimage is about: arriving at the holy place and allowing the old self to surrender to the truth that wants to enter.

"I BEGAN to have an idea of my life not as the slow shaping of achievement to fit my preconceived purposes, but as the gradual discovery and growth of a purpose which I did not know," Marion Milner writes in *A Life of One's Own*.

What is my purpose? What use my tools, my skills, my power? To ask these questions is transformational work. It is about creating one's own sacred destination, the holy city in which one wishes with all one's heart to arrive and to dwell.

My life has changed in ways I could never have imagined. I will always be a teller of stories. But where once I saw my role as helping to support women's movement out of our peculiar stagnant chrysalis into the flight of free beings, now I am more interested in the stories that arise from women's journeys into the interior, and from there into lives of transformed vision and authenticity. I am interested in a literature not of power, but of the choices women are making that extend the bounds of what we see as possible for our lives.

Camus once described the artist's role. He said that it is not to cause revolution, but to define what can follow from it. Imaginative revisioning, not insurgency, is our calling.

The work of creating new social organization, institutional change, and institution building, I leave to the likes of Femke, Ann Moritz, and so many others. My work, or the part of it that occurs at my desk, is to witness the meaning at the heart of these endeavors.

The first time someone served a cup of coffee in town, she turned on classical music and hung up a few pieces of art to complete the experience. She was being entrepreneurial, yes. But she was also tending to the native soul of the place.

I know of another woman who collects chipped china cups from flea markets and recycling bins and uses them as pots in which to give gifts of seedlings.

My purpose in writing about these and other women is to join their stories of individual transformation into a larger story of quiet cultural change, change that is being written by women on the script of history even as we sit here.

Meaning needs to be identified and depicted from time to time, or else we tend to lose the thread.

In her wonderful book *Composing a Life*, the anthropologist Mary Catherine Bateson points out that individual stories, like the testimonies of the medieval pilgrims, become something more when they are repeated. They become our modern myths of return and transformation.

"Women today, trying to compose lives that will honor all their commitments and still express all their potentials with a certain unitary grace, do not have an easy task," she writes. "It is important, however, to see that, in finding a personal path among the discontinuities and moral ambiguities they face, they are performing a creative synthesis with a value that goes beyond the merely personal. We feel lonely sometimes because each composition is unique, but gradually we are becoming aware of the balances and harmonies that must inform all such compositions. Individual improvisations can sometimes be shared as models of possibility for men and women in the future."

As I proceed through the streets of my town, my city, my far-flung relationships, gathering stories and cups of cappuccino, I try to do for others what I have so much needed to have done for me. I am trying to validate the works of ordinary women who are struggling to create a new reality, one that dignifies the spirit as it also insists upon the vital wisdom of the body; one that seeks to unite the ways of the earth to those of the mind, and life's daily path to its ultimate destination. Sabbath ways. These things cannot be divided.

Someday, I will venture farther afield in my search for such stories. But for now, the local scope of my endeavor fits my requirements for measure and balance, so essential to maintaining one's purposes.

Maintenance, meaning, measure — and available energy.

No one ever talked to us about limits when we were young. We wouldn't have listened. Limits seem such a compromise when one is twenty. But without boundaries and clear supporting structures, we grow formless. We lose a sense of the center. And without a center, we cannot have a "way."

Last night, I woke and went down into the dark living room. The moon had found one of my favorite pots, the raku jar, sitting low and sturdy on the mantel. It reminds me of the stone wall in New Hampshire that year in and year out has supported the wild raspberries that grow unrestrained among the roses. The wall will need mending in the warm season or the berries will eventually cease to ripen, choked by the more aggressive goldenrod and mint.

My journey has provided me with numerous metaphors of restoration, of mending and restitching a kind of wholeness into my life that was lost to many years of invasive things. From this place of arrival, I want to return to the broken walls, the flawed foundations of my generation's ideals. How might they be mended to provide good walls in a late season? For the flowers are still bright on the aging vines, still wild, still dazzling, reaching with every fiber of their remaining strength for the whole life they were born to experience.

NOW I EXTINGUISH my candle and go out on the deck. I take in the incredible beauty of creation in front of me, and like a loved one's greeting, the words of Proust come to mind once again:

"We must rediscover that reality from which we become separated as the formal knowledge we substitute for it grows in thickness and imperviousness, and which quite simply is our life."

At midlife, I have found my life and my purpose as a woman. As a pilgrim, I have discovered a reality whose nature is sacred and whose sacredness must be honored with balance, measure, and reverence. I have learned that such a life is simply not possible without a community of fellow travelers. And like the woman of my dream so many years ago, I know that my most important task is to hold these truths at the ever-unfolding center of the story that is my life.

Community

TODAY, my son begins school.

I tossed all night, unable to sleep. Will he be held within the same kind of loving community he has known up until now? Will this enlargement of his universe feel as graceful as the unfurling of the garden's late poppies? Will his friends be as sweet and funny and bright as he is? How much have they learned of levels and degrees of association, of the ties between self and other, of love in its many forms?

After breakfast, we make the drive to the little red farmhouse less than a mile away, through whose silo door he will enter the world with his new red backpack and his pencil case, his little boy's sunny eagerness. In the little classroom, I watch him disappear into the loft and take refuge in a book once I have said goodbye. With difficult resolve, I move past the miniature stove and hutch with their plastic milk cartons and baby bottles, soothing replicas of the world from which he is about to be schooled in this first of many separations.

I walk back through the barnyard, past the hens and goats, and retreat to the main road, heavy with ambivalence.

IN MY OFFICE, my notes and my journal await me, and with them, my efforts to make sense of women's lives today.

I've wanted to believe that I could find the principles of a life in which the sight lines are clear, free of distraction within and without so that women can recognize the seasons of their lives, hear what they need to of their inner voices, and determine whether their path remains a true one or needs, in times of transition, to be redrawn, brought into true.

This morning, I push my papers aside and shut my eyes. As I wonder how my three-year-old will fare these three hours, I am aware that, like him, it is not my solitary efforts that move or change anything. I can no longer think of myself as a self-sufficient professional, nor even as a working woman whose life revolves around the stimulating and challenging ideas of colleagues.

No, it is my friends and neighbors and my spiritual community who are the true guardian angels of all that is dearest in my days now.

I know that if I were to call Anne right now, she would have soothing words of wisdom on this difficult morning. Several times a month, we get our coffee, crawl back into bed, shoo kids and husbands away, and for an hour, go deep. I met Anne when I needed to find ways of looking at the world through new eyes. We belonged to the same health club. She'd come north to attend photography school and was just beginning to make her way as a children's photographer.

Now that she has moved back south, across the six hundred miles that separate us, we still lead each other back to balance, sanity—home to ourselves. We range freely over career transitions, school crises, marital discord. But mainly we talk about our spiritual lives and the struggle to maintain a true center in the midst of all the energy bursting around us, demanding our presence and continuous response. Like a pair trying to fit together the pieces of a five-thousand-piece jigsaw puzzle, we share our wisdom and our weaknesses.

Such a friendship points the way to my best experience of community. It is utterly devoid of the dependency or manipulation or the taking for granted that bedevil less pure relationships. There is a freedom from possessiveness. We seem capable of respecting one another's very different lives and find in this a special frankness that sets our understanding at a keener pitch.

Closer to my day-to-day life, there are my neighbors Linda and Pam, and Pam's husband, Mitchell, the neighborhood mother's group—all of us to some degree raising our children together, giving them the common and precious experience of being known and loved by the extended family of the street.

The neighborhood mother's group is the closest thing in my life to Femke's women. Peer into any of our living-room windows at 5:30 in the afternoon and you'll find a few of us on the sofas, while the children stack bright rings and pull little trucks on the rugs below.

We listen to one another, make useful suggestions, seek advice, and ease for one another our often solitary enterprise. Out of these weekly gatherings have come all sorts of neighborhood ventures. When our schedules create child-care gaps, we pinch-hit for one another. We provide an hour's "stress relief," by taking the babies off one another's hands. We hold block parties, Christmas-carol sings, and the New Year's Eve party we recently attended, with babies in tow, down the street. We have even loaned our houses to the visiting relatives of the group over the holidays.

When I was a childless full-time professional, I used to think of such "mother times" as a nullity, a few idle hours of contentless chat in lives unmoored from the safe harbor of a worldly identity.

I have been chastened for my arrogance. The mother's group provides spiritual succor and mutual aid. It is one of the few places outside the family that reinforces a fragile identity. And, at a time in life when time is precious and scarce, it is one of the few venues in which I can sustain female friendships distinct from my career. As we travel from house to house each Friday morning, rotating the task of hostess, as we munch on bagels at Andrea's and fancy raisin rolls at Melissa's, we forge bonds of concern and mutual obligation that haven't failed us yet. Not once.

I could not get through my day, much less have made the kinds of changes that I have in my life, without them. Nor without my workshop with its many mentors, and my spiritual director, Lynn; without Ann and Femke, inspiring examples of creativity at work.

Indeed, much of what I thought I wanted, most of what I suspected that I needed to change, had been churning inside my head for years. It took the human ties to make it all seem possible, necessary, and sane.

THE OTHER NIGHT, we had dinner with M., an old colleague who's become a national celebrity for her spirited defense of feminism and of women's contentment with the working world. She'd just come from hawking her new book on a local talk show. Her current take, that the recent attacks on the working parent are in reality attacks on working mothers.

Over dinner, she insisted that women, and the family, are doing fine. She outlined the trend currents: so-and-so's book, so-and-so's reaction. Front-page stories in Newsweek, The New York Times Book Review.

While the rest of us go on with the real business of living, the gladiators like M. slug it out. The points of contention get shriller and shriller until they vanish again, absorbed into the backdrop of public discourse. Whatever truth emerges from these exercises is, at best, descriptive, not transformative. The movements, the legislative efforts, even the pressure brought to bear on the workplace to give women and men more flexibility, rarely, if ever, occur.

From the vantage point of midlife, I believe that we have moved beyond movements with regard to matters of women's quality of life. We have entered a place where large-scale "movements" and polemics don't—can't—produce the salient structures for change. What women today need and are seeking isn't a new set of workplace guidelines. It is spiritual support. Community.

We are hungry for a shared wisdom about what constitutes a "good life." We want workable concepts and strategies. And we want intimate companions with whom we can live—in depth, in balance, in right livelihood.

Most of us long to find such companions. And when we do, the mere fact of finding one another creates a locus of change, a minute spark of support that slowly but surely begins to mold the shape of one's life.

How does one go about finding those who are right for us? How do women build this kind of community? And how, through community, can we exert the leadership to express a new vision of the way life might be lived?

AS I HAVE LIVED with these questions these past three years, I have found more and more similarly engaged women who are orienting themselves around a new image of home. What is interesting is that this image of "home" is being reclaimed by women from many different walks and stations of life, including women who aren't mothers or even householders. My single women friends, for whom home is the apartment they use to do the laundry and pay the bills, are reaching out to make new kinds of "home." They are adopting children. They are moving in downstairs from married siblings. They are associating with religious orders, or joining art groups, the church choir.

Some are using the old-fashioned designation of neighborhood to reinvent the idea of home. As soon as a house becomes available, word goes out to the friends of those who live here. The newcomers want closer contact, deeper ties, backyard Rosh Hashanahs and Easter egg hunts that include the whole street. Moms who pick up one another's slack, shared piano teachers, sitters, daffodil bulbs, tree trimmers—all the support mechanisms that make life livable and dear. Such ties become the hub of commitments that tend to radiate out to the larger circumference of the community in many and diverse ways, into its singing groups, its art exhibits and classes, its political associations.

In other ways too, women are attempting to create a parallel reality to the one supplied by mass culture and corporate life. My monthly creative-play group is such a space. The local Episcopal church that allows women to run a weekly discussion and support group around parenting issues is such a place. I know of continuing meditation groups, even knitting circles, comprised of young thirty-somethings that serve the purpose of spiritual support.

These intentional groups differ from earlier large-scale models of "liberation." They are intimate, face-to-face communities. They are value oriented, nonhierarchical, and voluntary. They begin in tangential ways around a theme or project or issue, but always evolve to focus on personal change, the desire of their members to reclaim authentic relationships with self and others, with work of value.

These are the primary places of meaning, today's hearths, usually hidden from public view and even from casual conversation, where women and some men are turning to find sanctuary as they try to lay the foundation for lives that are more connected and alive. Like a good home, and few workplaces, these "homes" allow for silence, experimentation, mistakes, for honesty, rituals, and real discussion of values.

I glance at the clock. The morning has ended and it is justifiably close enough to pick-up time to fetch my son. More than anything else, my overlapping circles of community have held me through my sometimes difficult journey of change. I am so grateful for the seamlessness of it all—a seamlessness that I would never have imagined possible in this day and age from my desk in a cold professional season four years ago.

WE SIT ON THE ROCK that overlooks the farm stand on the other end of the property while he finishes a treat, a soft lemon sweet that he can reach by himself from inside a glass candy jar by the checkout counter. We have both survived the hours apart.

Until this year, I couldn't have known that the farm where I have walked and shopped for so many years, in whose woods I've contemplated, and from whose fields I've eaten corn, broccoli, apples, also is home to a preschool that would be my son's first home away from home.

On the margins of the mainstream, women today are trying to live lives that cut distinctly against the grain of individualism and materialism. They are discovering such lives and calling them home. Increasingly, more and more are joining them. These "havens," I suspect, will remain marginal. But this in no way diminishes their value.

We have only to look at the environmental movement, the organic food movement, or the reawakening of faith communities to see that cultural change almost always begins on an intimate scale in the lives of individuals engaged in real conversations about real issues.

TONIGHT, Pam and Mitchell arrive with Perry for dinner. Some nights, we go to their house. The evening meal now often is communal, as friends new and old come together to share our daily burdens and bread. At least twice a week, we open our doors, making a celebration of what used to be a woman's solitary task and modeling for the children a more generous, capacious sense of family. In these days when one adult or another inevitably needs to work late, this sort of sharing makes all the difference between sterile, minimalist dinner hours and the events that dinners are meant to be, times of good conversation, laughter, and bountiful food.

It is an evening of apple tarts and boys with sticky fingers who push. The mothers hold colored storybooks in one hand and glasses of wine in the other.

Spilling down from the crowded table, the children make small worlds with their napkins, using crackers as rugs, a few nuts as themselves. Then they slip away to a corner to hit one another, then reach up to mother, crying.

The golden tallow of the candles, blue jeans and plaid shirts, hushed exchanges, the call for more ice cream, dishes as escape.

No, don't go, I'll call you in the morning.

I tuck a happy boy into bed.

Now the house is quiet. Mark is not yet home, so I take a glass of wine out on the porch and watch the sunset. The night grows dark. I can see fireflies down in the lower part of the yard. Up above, I catch sight of a shooting star.

Among the many stories of success that we told ourselves at twenty, a night like tonight wasn't among them. Its cares would have been quite literally unimaginable.

But in my forties, the terms have shifted. And I find that the realm of life to which I most want to attend with love and sensitivity is right here, right now. It requires a working philosophy of interdependence in which no part becomes so overbearing that it threatens the delicate, the dependent, the new.

At an earlier stage, this meant fostering my marriage. Then, my career. Now, it means raising my child and becoming a more balanced and passionate person. The energy that I need is no longer purely intellectual or professional. It is hands-on, intimate, related, and practical.

My child needs to be fed, loved, raised well; my mind and sensibilities clear enough to work. If I don't see to it that these things are done, and done well, who will? I am grateful to a man like Mitchell, who gives of his presence at our dinner table, and to him and Pam both, who are willing to extend the exuberant energies of their family life to include us, when Mark isn't able to be home. These things matter a great deal.

So does the mother's group, the life of our street, and the personalities and undertakings of this place where I make my home, all extending outward like the spokes of a well-wrought web. Only as I participate passionately in every aspect of my life—as wife, mother, writer, friend, householder—do I discover life itself. And at the center of it all, my true work.

This is an idea that as a young feminist I could never have understood. The personal with its minutiae had no serious place in the mind's passions, no power to compete with the magnetism of social revolution, global change. But lofty global and social concerns have challenged me to uphold a worthy consistency in the present. In the process, a fundamental shift has taken place. If I could summarize, which is always dangerous business, I would say that I have shifted away from self and toward a deeper acceptance of mutuality and responsibility, toward community. And I find in this not personal diminishment, but a new and profound sense of possibility and hope.

While I cannot imagine myself surrendering the solitary world of my garden house to begin writing in the equivalent of a quilting bee or sewing circle, or even a painter's studio, each day these relationships are making me more aware of my place in the common soil. Becoming present to the very rooted, particular reality of my own life and that of my child has opened me to concerns I didn't have before. I find myself "in" the world more than I ever have been and discover in this a profound convergence between my deepest individual yearnings and those of the society in which I am challenged to live.

If the last great historic thrust of women's energy was to attain power, independence, and individual opportunity, then the next must be to reestablish meaningful connection, a paradigm of spiritual and physical health, of human wholeness. We need to swing the balance, pull ourselves back from the edge of radical individualism and isolation and the emptiness of arrogance.

This has been a season of learning where I belong, in the life of the particular. By tending to my soul, my loved ones, my real purpose—whether in the garden or at my desk or along the street, the work has begun to fit the time allotted; a wholeness from out of the clay and benedictions of real days.

Isn't this another way of answering the elusive feminist question: What do I mean, today, by success?

I'VE BEEN REREADING Madeleine L'Engle's *Circle of Quiet*. At one point, from the wisdom of age fifty-one, she writes,

This time in Crosswicks [her family's country home] is a respite, perhaps an irresponsible one, for in this brief time I am more aware of a baby learning a new word, of the splashing of the brook after a rain, of the *isness* of lying in our big four-poster bed on a night when I retire with the babies and watch the green fade from the trees which surround our windows . . .

In the past few years we have seen more violence and horror than we would have thought possible, and there aren't any signs that it is going to stop without a great deal of pain and anguish . . .

I do not think that it is naive to think that it is the tiny, particular acts of love and joy which are going to swing the balance, rather than general, impersonal charities . . . They may be as quiet as pulling a blanket up over a sleeping baby. Or as noisy as the night of trumpets and stars.

COMING TRUE

I sit in the white rocker while my son plays at my feet in the wading pool, fishing with his plastic octopus, lobster, and friends. I am recruited occasionally, but he is mainly content, as am I, embroidering an old piece, an image of the farms I remember from my beloved Ontario in winter.

The sun shifts; a cardinal calls to its mate. And soon the boy grows weary of distance. I find a slick body sidling up to me, pressing against my thigh, asking to take the needle and guide it himself, in and out of the cloth. For a few moments, we both become weavers. A needle, and then a pin, is stuck into my leg more often than I care to recall. The white floss lies forgotten, abandoned on the design.

I put the hoop aside and pull him onto my lap. He falls in readily, his head nestling in the collar of my neck, happy to have my hands warm him with their steady strokes. He smells of sun and dirt, sweat and small boy sweetness.

The light on his hair and across the magnificent whorls of down on his back is beautiful. I love the feel of him, his thighs and buttocks and perfect arches, his sweet shoulders and tilted neck.

We rock and I sing. Then, for no reason in particular I begin to recite a poem that I memorized when I was eight years old and staying at my best friend's beach house:

All to myself, I think of you
Think of the things we used to do
Think of the things we used to say
think of each golden yesterday.
Sometimes I sigh
And sometimes I smile,
But I keep each olden, golden while
All to myself.

He listens, his body soft in the deep warmth of sunlight; hearing the words, but not hearing them, just feeling the mood. We are one.

Through the long hours and days of growing into being mother and son, through the long night struggles, the sicknesses, through all the work of growing into wisdom, I come to myself in this moment in the garden. And I know, even as I record it, that this will be one of the holy hours that I will press into my own book of wisdom, a particle of perfection that I will bring out to warm myself on the solitary evenings to come when the sky and all but the lamp over my book will be dark to save on electricity, and all will seem so still and so silent and so past somehow, and I in it—waiting for I don't know what. I pray I will have the good heart and the courage to remember these years, these many and diverse moments of true connection, between the room and the garden, the flesh and the poem. This is heaven, as I have known it—undeserved, unhoped for, unimagined grace.

THREE

Toward Fifty

Seasons

THE CLAY POTS on my terrace stand in that dewy state of newly minted spring this morning as the sun climbs the railings. Yesterday was a tumble of plastic nursery packs, loose potting soil, muddy tools, and a still muddier boy, beside himself with the thrill of the garden hose.

By dinner, we were happily exhausted. The flurry of potting was over, and I had just enough energy left to sweep aside clods of dirt and shards of broken pots, wipe the table of scattered seeds, and sit down to sautéed sugar snap peas.

Soon, my terrace will be bursting with white petunias and silver dusty miller, hot red salvias and purple lobelia, splashes of pansies and trailing vinca. Come August, it will barely be able to contain all of this billowing, bee-beloved bounty. Then a frost will snap. The glory will fade. And for a season, we will feed on memory and dream. A cycle will have accomplished itself, and it is precisely this closure, this entirety, that I feel most privileged to witness (and where I can, to abet) on the threshold of midlife.

I go back in the house, pour my coffee, and take a seat by the window so I can continue to see the young seedlings while I write in my journal. I am no longer as awed by the obvious peaks of display as I am by the ways in which living things fulfill their particular destinies. With this at the forefront of my thoughts this morning, I suppose it is inevitable that I would ask myself what constitutes the completion of *our* human labors? In all their diversity, is there a common shape, like that of the hawthorn or the rose?

Day after day, I set down my thoughts, as other women set out surgical tools or prepare marketing reports or fold laundry. I suppose that I could liken these works to marigolds or garden-variety geraniums, naturally occurring productions that repeat themselves day in and day out once we've taken root and decided to develop in a certain direction.

But beneath the daily, weekly, monthly struggles, the miscarriages and the stillbirths, the sacrifices, compromises, and the bone-breaking labor of delivering them into the world, there is unfolding in us at every moment the deeper inner cycle of our life, of which we are but dimly aware. The truth is, we prefer not to know. We see the trees lose their leaves, the flowers their vital colors, vines wither. We observe only loss and the chill remains of a cold, hollow season. (Who are we to guess at the memory of plants?) So we avert our gaze, preferring to prolong the high season of bloom as long as we can, extending it, urging our younger powers beyond their natural season, never realizing that there may be other powers that await us if only we don't refuse the Indian-summer promise of intensification, passion, and completion.

The fulfillment of my tomatoes consists in more than their blossoms, and deep inside I know so does mine. I want to know what the terms of my particular fulfillment *are*, and this morning, I

suspect that this requires me to see my life, a woman's life, in much
the way I do my plants, as a succession of seasons.

Certainly in cultures that hew closer to the wisdom of the earth
and the lessons of nature than we, people have done just this for centuries. Youth was the time to take root, to learn the ways of the tribe,
its myths and terms of mastery, whether one grew up in aboriginal
New Guinea or Indiana farm country. Young adulthood, the twenties and thirties were, and still are, marked by feats of self-sufficiency
and achievement, and the taking up of one's work in the world. This
is the period of fertility and productivity, of blossom and promise,
that by midseason enters a prolonged stage of stability and profusion. Careers are solidified, households settled, community work
expanded. Up through this "summer" season of life, our modern life
more or less conforms to the pattern of cultures past. It is in the next
stage, the stage of the harvest, that we radically diverge.

Women in most traditional cultures continue to contribute to
the planting and the weaving, the mundane tasks of survival as the
harvest season approaches. But there is a distinct shift in the quality
of their work. At midlife, their contribution can no longer be that of
the energetic worker bee, the star poppy. It is expected—indeed, is
needed—to embody a higher level of articulation. They become
the master teachers and the healers. From technical proficiency,
their reach is expected to extend to the intuitive; from how-to
knowledge to wisdom, from the *matter* of life to its mysteries. They
are expected to have matured to the point where they bear this
sagacity like a good crop, not merely for the edification of their own
families, or for personal prestige, but for the good of the tribe, with
an attitude of generosity and service toward future generations.

In midlife Bantu tribal rites, for example, if a woman has been
especially virtuous and wise, she is awarded the prized medicine bag.
Henceforth, she has the power to heal. In other cultures, women at
midlife begin to officiate over rituals and are, by extension, also

given the power to heal. The bearers of the harvest become the source of continuing wisdom for other adults and for the young who are being raised in the sacred ways of the tribe.

We moderns, to the contrary, try to prolong our summer bloom as long as we can. And because women's life patterns have come to so closely resemble men's, we have, in addition, tended to minimize the pivotal events of fertility and growth (childbirth and menopause being only the most obvious) that differ from men's and, by extension, the wisdom associated with them.

As I sit here sipping my cooling coffee, I can't help but wonder if we haven't unconsciously eliminated the harvest season of life because we can no longer think outside the box of continuous summer? Because we can no longer imagine a phase of life that contains new and different works, works that would require us to turn away from being the makers of blossoms and become instead the bearers of fruit?

I hear the gate click shut next door. It is my neighbor, Susan, and her eight-year-old daughter, rushing off to school. Two nights ago on one of those perfect spring evenings, they joined us on the back deck for dinner. Susan's mood was noticeably subdued.

"You look down," I commented over our chicken and pasta.

She nodded.

"I was talking to a friend of mine the other day," she answered. "A surgeon with two children. She said to me, 'You know, Susan, I've studied and studied, and worked and worked. And now, I want to stop.'"

Susan, who just turned fifty, looked at me ruefully. "Those of us who waited a long time to have our children can't afford to stop."

"Maybe your depression is telling you that you need to grow in new ways."

"Yes," she agreed. "I *do* want to grow now, and in different ways. *I just feel that I can't.*"

As I listen to her car pull away and know that she faces another long day of hospital rounds and sick children before she returns home to her daughter late tonight, I think that if we were to reclaim our authentic life stages as women, perhaps she *could* grow. The "I can't" of women on the upward ascent of our careers put us in danger of very nearly losing the chance to know the joy of children and the more abundant selves that parenthood brings. Now, the "I can't" of a continuous summer mentality threatens to cut short the midlife time of wisdom, of the harvest so crucial to our capacity to understand our life's meaning.

Another, similar conversation comes to mind as I write. Last month, an old high-school friend came to town for a weekend without her husband and three children in tow. Mary has spent the last twenty years as a full-time wife and mother. She has loved every minute of it.

"Amazing though it is to admit it," she told me as we shared a turkey club sandwich in a posh hotel lobby downtown. "Motherhood really *was* my calling. But the kids are getting older. They need me more in some ways, less in others. I see Beth back in graduate school, working and happy, and I find myself thinking, 'There's got to be more than Junior League.'"

This truth is that our lives as women—our needs, our capacities, our creativity—are seasonal. Wholeness, fulfillment, even success evolves for us over a lifetime. This is a fundamental reality of the feminine, and we women need to develop a vision of our lives that is large enough to honor it, if we are to succeed at being more than endless blooms in the world of men—if we are to experience our own form of wholeness.

THE DAY I PLANTED a rosemary in the earth of my rocky New England, I became a more grounded creature. Each morning, I trekked out with my watering can. I stood in the winking dawn and felt the crazy, spinning earth, on which I'd scrambled just to keep myself upright all these years, slow nearly to a stop. The garden became my great teacher and healer, an apt and ever-deepening symbol of what it is to be a woman.

I learned that a good garden is about pattern, a well-thought-out coherence of elements chosen for color, variety, shape, and blooming times. The peonies will explode, the golden lily roust itself beside the bleeding hearts—then out come the annuals planted for variety: bachelor buttons and nasturtiums. Sometime around August, the hydrangea will blow puffs of rose white into the air, which the sedum will echo in its lovely, bruised rose. Then it will all turn to fire and gold, fixed for a few brief days in the amber of autumn, and on to fallen leaf.

As my own summer begins to fade, I feel a different energy begin to make itself felt. I feel a turning, within. I am no longer facing so exclusively outward, reaching for the sun. Instead, I move inward. I feel that I am standing on the threshold of unknown mysteries. Where for so many years I have tried to send forth showy blossoms, now I am changing into something else.

All summer long, at a hidden, cellular level, the trees and herbs on my property are monitoring the hours of sun energy they receive, the ambient temperature of the night air, preparing themselves for the transformations of fall. This is work that occurs in a darkness as deep as the oak's roots. It is as ancient as time. Without it, the garden would be unable to perform the extraordinary metamorphosis that it does—green to ruby, bloom to pod.

If the garden is a true teacher, it tells me that women too need a period of darkness, time with the invisible forces in our lives, to prepare ourselves for the harvest. In traditional societies, such a time of deep and silent preparation was the norm.

The Bible describes one such custom, the "Sabbath of Sabbaths." The Sabbath of Sabbaths, or the Jubilee Sabbath, as it was also known, was a two-year period from a woman's forty-ninth through her fiftieth year, just before the great physical shift of menopause. During the Jubilee Sabbath, she retreated somewhat from her normal labors and looked inward. It was considered a sacred time, a time for her to explore the years' accumulated wisdom and meditate on the ways in which she might employ it most effectively in the next and final phase of her life.

For most of us, a Jubilee Sabbath isn't possible. But even to take an hour a week as "jubilee time," in the garden, alone with a thought-provoking book, or in meditation, would be a revolutionary act toward reclaiming a season long neglected, and with it our opportunity to grasp our life's call to completion.

Perhaps I need to consider this time with my journal, my time in the garden, as my own small form of jubilee time—the private, invisible places where I am preparing for the season ahead. Here, I look back and inward more than I look ahead. I am reminded that nothing feeds a garden so well as what has already gone before it. The dead leaves and compost of seasons past make the soil lighter, richer, more nutritious, and this, in turn, improves the quality of what it next sends forth. Given enough air for circulation, enough water for its essences to mingle and render, the old thus becomes the ground for the wholly new. Ideally, what we accomplish in one season prepares us for the work that follows in the next, the inner movements and turnings eventually manifesting in a graceful synthesis, a well-evolved form.

The ancient symbol of this process was the circle, in many cultures the symbol of life itself. As I stand at the start of a new and unknown season, I want to complete my own circle with courage, vividness, and intensity. For the first time in my life, it is absolutely vital to me that I accede to the authority of my beliefs and proceed from them, and that I choose undertakings based on a realistic assessment of my energies. In our society, this is the ultimate risk, to let one's life and work issue from the few things that we really believe in; to do what we can and no more. But it is also the ultimate faithfulness.

I know that all transformation involves struggle—against unknowing, intellectual roadblocks, life circumstances, exhaustion, and the overcoming of our own insufficiencies, inner doubts, lack of commitment, discipline, concentration. This is why we need to honor the invisible work of the seasons in us. We need our hours of quiet, invisible preparation, gathering the cell memories, the wisdom of the spirit, to see us through.

The purples and yellows of my spring garden are in thrall to the dynamic tension of becoming that we as women need to reclaim. If we could fashion a new vision of our life's seasons, we will have prepared the soil for the harvest. And if we can do *this*, I believe that we can begin to imagine a world in which women would be able to do many more things and with far greater freedom than we can now. We would be able to move in and out of various types of work—professional, volunteer, child rearing, creative, caring for the sick and the elderly—*according to our life phases*, without a sense of punishment or victimization for the variety of works that we feel called over a lifetime to perform.

This is a mere cutting, a slender slip of green, that I take from the rosemary and offer to the water. We might begin by learning from the traditions of other women, living and dead, who have lived out a fuller, more culturally sanctioned harvest season. We might find those who are writing and thinking about these matters from an economic and cultural perspective, in order to better understand what needs to be done to change the patterns of sustenance that we, in a culture of summer, adhere to.

And then we need to return to our gardens. We need to cultivate them in the manner that is unique to each of us. In this kind of a garden, this kind of a life, one's own arrangement is the "right" one, and we are not so much absorbed in grasping it lest it get away from us, as in letting it reveal all of its beauties from its first green to its final bronze, making a place for the fostering darkness, for the hour of waiting, that precede metamorphosis.

Perhaps it will be a new work. A new community project. A new job. An adjustment of working terms or environment or relationships to better suit the selves we now want and need to give to the world.

When we choose our gardens at last, they will lead us into the fertile darkness. And in the quiet hours of our hearts, they will reveal to us the true harvest of our labors.

Making Home

WE HAVE COME AWAY to the shore with as little as we can manage: sand pails and sun lotion and a change of underwear apiece. We want a few days of stripping down to the bones of ourselves.

Each morning after breakfast is the same. We rummage for shells, sing a little, decorate wet sand with stones. Then we stop for lemonade and strawberries, sorting, as we munch, through our latest booty, laying out, naming, and finally placing things into a bucket with the intention of carrying home a collection, something shapely and complete.

It is ten o'clock, and we have begun our sand castles. As my son scrapes and shapes and excavates for a foundation, I begin my own beside him. I advance to the outer walls of the first story and stop, careful not to get too far ahead, not to move too quickly, so as not to discourage him. When he wanders off again in search of more algae, egg pods, broken shells, I sit back, free to think.

Last night in the borrowed bed of a rented bungalow, I dreamed of a new home. Dreams about homes are never neutral events for me. I've dreamed of dungeons in which I've been trapped in the role of domestic slave. I've dreamed of penthouses in which I've been forced to play the eternal social hostess. I can't say which was a worse nightmare. This dream was different. It was a detailed, vivid, joyful dream. The rooms of this home were large, the views good. It was a place where I could live abundantly.

Now the gulls careen at the crashing surf, mining for hermit crabs that will scurry for cover once the action moves out. Until recently, I lived like such a crab. I was one of so many who in the seventies joined consciousness-raising groups where we sat in one another's living rooms, in coffeehouses, in college dorms, defying any architecture—social or physical—that would confine us as homemakers.

For us, the only acceptable "home" was the tide of the world itself; our work, the world's work. Children were being burned to death from Northern Ireland to South Africa. The rain forest was diminishing daily. Our sisters were continuing to be subjected to torture and domestic imprisonment. How could we do otherwise, we asked ourselves, without seriously expecting any rejoinder. Our temporary, shifting "rooms of our own" would support us in the spartan, provisional ways that we required to meet the world and our work in it. The choice seemed so obvious. We needed nothing more.

My son returns. He has found a wonderfully sodden mat of kelp and eggs, a whole colony of dogfish, one might guess, and my reverie is temporarily brought back down to gritty earth. With the termination of the nap hour, more children have arrived, and the morning's castle now rises gradually into life. Walls and pools, roads and resident cat figures take their place under the hands of eight or ten urchins—a whole neighborhood, patched together from the goodwill of little strangers.

LATER, back in the cottage, I prepare a good, simple meal. After a warm bath, I am in bed early. I read, then allow myself a delicious spell of unhurried letter writing before drifting once more into dreams.

It occurs to me as I turn out the light that without being entirely conscious of it I have been acquainted with last night's messengers for some time. The fact is, that while we modern women start with a room, we must end up with a home.

After years of living like migratory creatures, alighting where life speaks to us, then moving on, most of us come to a place where we seek to stay put, to live what we have learned on some kind of home ground. We want to create a domicile that is both physically and emotionally hospitable, deeper and more integrating than simply the next project or the next creative endeavor can possibly be. The fruits of our journey cry out for more enduring form.

Women can lose themselves in many ways in this world—abstraction, addiction, overwork—and call it "good work." But we regain ourselves in only one, and this is by returning to home ground and growing outward again from the nourishing privacy provided by a composition that is uniquely ours.

At their best, our homes are the places where we are most able to be ourselves. They are where our varied parts—our laughter, our dirty socks and burned beans, our poems and our unpaid bills—are able to coexist easily without competition in the hierarchy of the self. Even in the midst of pressure and stress, when we are truly at home, we can find a corner, a half hour, to sit and simply breathe, to find the still point within.

This still point is a daily requirement. It is every bit as important as our rightful place in the public sphere. Without it, we become stretched too thin. We crack under the externally imposed terms of our lives. We need to reclaim the right to the center; without it, we are homeless, adrift in the provisional dwellings tossed up by the tide.

As a younger woman, I was fascinated by the female cultural heroes of the nineteenth and early twentieth centuries. Edith Wharton the woman intrigued me more than did her novels. Eleanor Roosevelt intrigued me for far more than her political courage, as did Edith Stein, the Jewish convert and Holocaust victim who spent her preconvent days writing about the needs of women.

I maintained, and still do, the attractive impression of their sallying forth into public life from profoundly satisfying private worlds of their creation, worlds anchored in a feminine interiority and decorum that contained ample space and time for reflection, learning, and debate.

It seems to me inevitable that once we are drawn to such women in their public thought, we long to know how they fostered and kept themselves at home. The glib reply is that most of them had servants, which enabled them to accomplish all that they did. But this doesn't obscure my sense that in the lives of the women many of us choose as our models, an ineffable harmony bound the public and the private realm. Further: that if we are truly to understand the power of their public voices, we must understand their private worlds as well.

Most of us as early feminists had the idea that time and energy spent in making one's home a hospitable and soul-nourishing place—simple and streamlined when we were alone, more commodious and elaborate when it became the place we shared with others—was a drain on our productivity.

In midlife, I've discovered that just the opposite is true.

A woman must know her threshold. She must know it in order to bless it when she leaves it and to recognize it when she returns. As life comes and goes across it, she must exercise the care of a hospitable but cautious householder: to be willing to welcome the guests, to rearrange the furnishings, to mend and change as conditions require. And she must be able, when necessary, to shut the door, change the lock, and sit in her garden until a new wind revives her.

Many of the women I've met who have scaled back their public lives and retreated to home or garden have been looking to retrieve the reality of this threshold. They've needed to pass from the realm of competitive individualism into an interior that is alive with something else entirely. And this "something else"—restorative calm, gentle pleasure—they have needed to recover from the storeroom of memory. They have mined their individual memories, sifted and gleaned from the collective memory of grandmothers and aunts, the old stories of the feminine, whose booty must be collected, renamed, and reshaped to meet the needs of our modern lives.

The something that they seek, and that I seek in coming to this most private spot on the shore, is the legitimate and vital presence of the "heart(h)" self, the maker of genuine home. We need the sense that she makes of things, and the fact that, mysteriously, she does, ever and again, make sense.

We must be free to leave our homes, to risk and achieve and lose, in the larger corridors of the world. We know that to hang back in the lovely order of our interior spaces would ultimately doom us to lives of sterility. But we also know that it is only from this heart(h) place that we are able to move out in meaningful ways.

Moreover, we know that the division between hearth and the world, private and public, is an arbitrary and largely artificial one. A home is never a wholly private affair. If it is interesting, it bristles with variety, with hospitable entrances and interesting wings. While it is the external mechanism for keeping our inner wholeness alive and well, it is first and foremost, as anyone who has realistically grappled with the challenge of making home can attest, a web of relationships.

A good home allows us to grow, to put on additions, to shut down wings and clear out closets, to shape a life in the world that is coherent with our private truths. As the source of a woman's stamina and insight, her compassion and strength, the home may well be the guiding image that, in spite of ourselves, we were seeking in those consciousness-raising sessions of so long ago. Our homes may be what we need to reclaim today, where feminism leaves off.

The castle that I began earlier on the beach was much more peopled than my actual home has ever been. I made a larger footprint, allowed for more and more varied spaces.

I can imagine a day when I will return to solitude, not to the searching solitude of my twenties, but to a self who is less anchored in place, is more mobile and transparent. But for now, I know that to live as I must, I need to position myself in the complex truths of the dream, with its peopled spaces, its overflowing rooms, its vital and demanding proportions.

YESTERDAY, our last day here, we built an entire city in sand. It was a sort of prehistoric settlement that, by the time it was finished, extended five feet by ten and was encompassed on all sides by ramparts. Inside stood a tiered Mayan castle surrounded by a seaweed forest. The forest itself was occupied by the tower of the resident wizard. To the south stretched the peaked homes of the villagers, arrayed in lovely order: first, the great house, then the fields, and beyond, a magnificent goddess figure in relief, looking for all the world like the yeast figures the ancient Greek women used during their annual fertility rites. Last came the crude huts of the outlanders and five sand towers intended to represent the spiritual axis of the community. Not a church, exactly, but close enough.

It was the only sand play we've done entirely without tools, plastic shovels, or pails, and it was by far the finest. From our hands and a few bits of broken shell, some semblance of civilization, some articulation of an idealized and entirely subconscious order, emerged.

We let it be, with as little fanfare as we'd begun. We just stopped working on it. The boys went swimming. I returned to my perch up the way. Beachcombers stopped from time to time to admire it. One little one couldn't resist stomping on the five towers, darting back and forth gleefully with each strike. No one, least of all us, tried to stop him.

Finally, it was time for us to leave. As we crested the rise of the dunes and headed down the other side, my son looked back and said with a sigh, "Mommy, I hope our city doesn't break."

I explained the wonder of the tides that sweep everything away, leaving us free to begin again.

"You mean, to build *exactly* the same city, Mommy?" he asked with yearning, running alongside me.

This is the way it always is at the beach. Sand is the earth's great reminder of impermanence. Its resident creatures, the crabs and snails, bury deep within, or abandon their abodes. At low tide, the strand is a kingdom of deserted dwellings; at high, the ruins of human hands.

Finally, our stay too is impermanent. We leave and return to another world and another season of growth.

But each time, if the process has been true, we shed a dwelling that has grown too small for us. Each time, we peel away protective habits, conventions old or new. We come away more at home with ourselves.

Once we modern women attend to the neglected homes within us, we are in a position to address their disrepair in the culture as a whole, tangibly supporting other women who are beginning to make home again and speaking with greater insight to the pervasive existential crisis of homelessness around us. In articulating a reorientation that values homemaking in the best sense of the word, perhaps we can bring to the cultural discourse a perspective that is desperately needed if we are to build a more compassionate, civilized world.

Along with the shovels and notebooks, our newfound shells and sand-filled pens, I carry back with me the heart(h) self of new acceptance. In middle age, I have become a homemaker.

Interdependence

THE OLD COWBELLS and prize ribbons still hang proudly just inside the entrance to the barn, though it has been a generation since anything like the practices of rural agriculture have been employed on this land. The milk conveyor still runs through what is now the "shop," though it is full of flashlights and batteries, Christmas ornaments and flower vases.

These days, the farm, hidden away in a village of seven hundred in the heart of the White Mountains, is a retreat for busy family members from faraway cities. But for all that has been lost of its earlier purposes, it continues to revive in us a searching awe, a current of unwavering awareness of our intricate and irreducible reliance upon nature.

From time to time, an organic garden has flowered here. We see moose, search for deer scat by the lower pond, watch the shifting flash of storms and the quiet sunsets. And somehow we are cleansed by it all.

This morning, the meadow is exquisite with life. Swallowtails, coppers, and azures are dipping and feeding. A gusty breeze is turning the fields into a rippling pelt of green. Birds—some that I know, others not—spiral and patrol under cloudless skies. It is a morning of ease and glory.

I sit against the barn and feel its heat slowly enter my body. The privilege of being in this place, in the presence of such a view, is greater than I can convey. Remote from the house, phones, interruptions, I try to settle into a state of simple awareness amid the oak fern and ryegrass that skim the shadows along the edge of the woods.

I move a few stones around on the boards of the weathered porch, shift and rearrange them until I find a pattern that is pleasing. Then I shift them again, letting my various jangling thoughts enter into their figures as they may and then depart: the nature of my current life, which is at once so intensely private and so astonishingly busy; the question of the work to be done next, now that my community portraits are finished for the time being. After a half hour or so, all of these thoughts quiet in me and I am left with the simple pleasure of handling stones, their heft and texture, and the residue of wakeful attention that rises when I am able to arrive at such a state within.

I find these days that in such moments of reflection a certain question arises again and again.

How is it that we humans behave with such obliviousness to our interdependence with nature and with one another? We see the facts of it daily in our parks and gardens, on our weekend walks by the shore or in the woods. We know its vital necessity in the healthy raising of a child, its role in the preservation of the family, its place in the well-being of the individual adult.

How then do we manage to live with so very little of it in what motivates and orders our daily lives? We rely on others, paid professionals, to do the works of binding, nurturing, healing, and caretaking that many of us these days consider quite frankly beneath us. The real answer, if we consider all of the loneliness, alienation, and dysfunction that attend this way of life, is—not well at all.

What would it take for us to return to an ethos of genuine interdependence, to a world in which the fragile, the evanescent, the spirit among (and within) us were as well-loved and tended as the predator, the competitively fit? Are there instances of communities that still live this way, whose rites and practices might open us to a new way of our own?

I am drawn back to this question, over and over again. A small caterpillar lands on my hand. It is green, with a round gold head and copper tail—a silver azure. It is looking for food that I cannot give. I put him down and let him meander across the page.

He will eat and eat and eat until the time comes for him to transform himself. Nearly all of the strength and stamina he will need to accomplish his mature labors depends upon the eating that he does now, since a butterfly does not eat solids, but relies instead on sips of nectar for brief bursts of energy.

As he has reached the edge of the page, I pick him up and set him down on a blade of grass. In pleasure, he wraps himself around it, like a hug.

I soon lose sight of him. But his airborne relations once more command my captive admiration. They are almost too delicate, too beautiful, to have any function other than to add their pulsing colors to a summer's day. They are the grace notes of the garden. Like floating petals, they seem; beauty pure and simple, sprung free, unloosed from any toiling, earthbound care.

Yet they are not unloosed at all. Their work is indispensable. It is they who ensure the flower's transformation to fruit, from a quickly fading beauty to a deeper and more essential force of nourishment.

Beautiful though they are, their work is humblingly mechanical. They ferry bits of fertile powder from tiny cup to cup on airborne legs, all the while avoiding the voracious beaks of sharp-eyed, competent birds. Butterflies toil ceaselessly in the sun and rest in the shade. And they do all this with a dazzling lightness and fleetness of duration that painters have tried to represent from the beginning of time.

Born not of the earth itself, but essential to it, it seems to me this morning that they hold in perfect equipoise the interplay of purpose, beauty, and meaning that is our highest potential as human beings.

Yesterday, at the Audubon sanctuary not far from home, I attended a class on butterflies. Any number of times, our instructor stopped and captured something for our examination, and any number of times, we heard about the cannibalistic and predatory habits of these beautiful creatures. About larvae who eat one another the moment they are born, about birds contentedly chewing the bodies of monarchs and casually spitting out the wings.

One of our group was an older woman. She was somewhat halt, and as we traipsed into the woods, she reached down for a makeshift walking stick. At each stop on the way, she required increasingly substantial support. Finally, she was making her way with the group on the crutch of a bough. It seemed only natural, an integral quality of the afternoon, that one or another of us should stay behind the others and help her while the rest ran to catch the words of our indefatigable, net-waving instructor.

We too are cannibals and predators. But what saves us are the occasions when our work, like the butterfly's—our caretaking and nursing, our teaching, parenting, gardening—becomes distilled fruitfulness, when our creativity and generosity act to affirm our interdependence, in the name of a culture based on the same.

Beauty and intimacy anchored in time and place often seem to us incidental, ornamental, to the main event of our ambition and quest for success. But kill the particular—the plant, the connection with a child, the friendship, the promise—and we kill the dance. We doom all work, all human culture, because we have cut ourselves off from the one enduring source of tenderness and joy that is our only hope of self-transcendence. In the swallowtail, in the almost heartbreaking beauty of the dove-colored mourning cloak, we learn that in our most vulnerable creatures, our most vulnerable selves, lies the missing piece of the soul.

IN THIS WHITE MOUNTAIN VILLAGE, things happen, as it were, by the consent of the collective. Rugs are braided, woods timbered, and fires put out, together. When a child was orphaned some time back, a neighboring couple took him in and raised him. These days, they voluntarily keep house for a disabled man and his wife. When a person is widowed, comfort and help come in as many ways as there are wayfarers. And each August, tractors, horses, carts, and antique bicycles are festooned with bunting and family regalia and roll their way past the post office and the general store in celebration of this way of life to the delight of the small but loyal crowd, neighbors all.

All is far from perfect in this town. Acts of predation and cannibalism have transpired here, impulse has governed personal conduct with as much hapless chaos as it does elsewhere. But the rites of particularity give folks here the ability to ask for and obtain forgiveness, to sustain love, to know one another, and to transform their labors into sense, service, beauty.

Back home, I look to the neighbors with whom I can entrust my son when emergency strikes. I look to my local farm stand to produce food according to organic notions of interdependence. I look to my community of faith to affirm the humanly divine dance of unity.

I know now that work that is nourishing in a real sense is work that sustains our interdependence, in the ways we relate to one another, in our habits, in the gestures by which we convey love. I know that the source of tenderness and joy, without which no work can in any real sense be satisfying, is not the monumental, but the particular, not the "big splash," but that which is nourished over time.

It isn't glamorous, but it is indispensable. It is the work not of the needy caterpillar, but of the evanescent butterfly. And so this morning, I watch them closely, a painter without a brush, trying to trace their dance onto memory so that I may come to know it as my own.

Integration

EVERY AUGUST for years now, I put the finishing touches on a fruit compote that becomes the pièce de résistance of our Christmas feast. It is a grand composition when done. But it builds through the summer months from wonderfully simple fare. As each fruit of the season comes into peak, several perfect specimens are tossed into the massive mason jar that otherwise waits out its time on a shelf in the cellar.

First come the strawberries. Next raspberries, then cherries and peaches.

The calendar is much the same as when I was a child and sat behind my father on the tandem bike as we rode through the early Canadian morning to the farm stand down the way. Then come the plums and finally, in August, the blueberries.

In with each fruit goes a cup of sugar and one of brandy. Then it is left to ferment in an out-of-the-way place where no careless hand groping for a tool, no small traveling sword in search of Beowulf, will disturb it. Left, that is, except for the one addition that I will make today—a late-season MacIntosh picked yesterday on a rolling hill in the country near Groton.

I descend to the dark cellar, pass the clay pots and planters stacked in the cool now for a long season, and the garden tools that have been oiled and put away. High up on a wooden shelf sits the mason jar, its sweet contents dim. Carefully, I pull it down and carry it past the silent denizens of summer up into the sun-splashed autumn kitchen.

Its color no longer resembles any of those of its ingredients—the bold red and stout blue of the berries, the saffron of peaches, the amber of brandy. These short months have worked their subtle alchemy. And to it the apple is about to submit, joining the old wine that stirs like jeweled velvet in the depths of the jar.

When I first began making the compote, I simply bought fruit in season at the grocer's. Now, each comes from a particular provenance, a distinct garden or mountaintop or orchard, chosen over years of fruit picking for the bonds of affection and memory that have grown up around each one. The strawberries are a blend of our own backyard alpines and those we pick at a berry festival in nearby Weston. The raspberries come from our neighbor Grace's canes; the peaches from New York; the cherries from our annual visit to Canada; and last but not least, the blueberries from Foss Mountain in New Hampshire. In this way, the geography of our intimate world is represented—the year, as it were, recomposed for review at the great midwinter feast of celebration and new life that we share each December. The fruits mingle their flavors and chemistries until the whole sweet, fermented porridge provides a pleasure both present and past, as we reminisce about the source of each successive citizen of the brew.

Yesterday, when we set out in search of apples, really *was* the final day of the harvest. We were among the last pickers at the

orchard. From a distance, we could see no color on the rows of low-
growing trees. As we drove in and scanned the hills for winks of red,
we feared that we might actually have been too late. But once we
climbed the rise, our sacks in hand and our picnic lunch in a knap-
sack on my back, we discovered an entire section that had been
overlooked by earlier day-trippers. Small, hard, and intense, the
Macs were delicious, and we felt as profligate as the first creatures
in Paradise plucking samples and biting in. Greedily we gathered,
as if the apples were days, or rubies, or the lost secrets of time itself.

The hill on which we worked under warm sunlight couldn't
have been lovelier. It was a day of storybook beauty. Below us
spilled a dazzling spread of maple, oak, and birch, their colors
dwarfing the small town beneath their canopy, all except the single
steeple that pierced through, thrusting white into the perfect blue
beyond.

As I rested from gathering my fourth quart bag, I too felt like a
tree late discovered, late blessed. My son romped like a joyful
puppy, and as I reached for my journal to sketch the scene, I was
diverted into one of those contemplative streams that sweep life's
blessings to the fore with all the vividness of the surrounding leaves.

Surely I, who had abjured the whole notion of motherhood for
twenty years, did nothing to deserve such a sweet-tempered son.
Nor as patient a mate as I've had standing by me through the fluc-
tuations of weather my flowering has required, trusting that in the
end I would find the right habit of growth, the roots to stay the journey. Nor the friends who've caught and held me fast when I've
needed their ties and supportive wisdom.

As the momentum of age gathers in my own approaching season
of harvest, I am aware of so many gifts. Often it seems to me these
days as if the blessings of my life, and yes its trials, are setting as fruit.
As if my awareness of life's peaking has brought them out, to be
plucked and tasted, to be distilled into an essence—an image, a

lesson, a shape—through which I can both celebrate them and all that has gone before now, and be carried into another life, beyond them. These fruits are telling me that I am nearing the end of my time as root, trunk, and limb for my son and my husband, that I am transforming from leaf, flower, and sap into something else, something that is yet to come.

I say the "momentum of age." Yet the years since I turned forty have felt more like a slowing down. I have experienced greater inwardness, more concentrated energies, and this has enabled me to walk through my days more alert to their renderings. I feel like a well-seasoned root stock, sending out late fruit. And if I were to choose which fruit, I would be the one that I love the best and the one, perhaps not coincidentally, that occasioned man's first loss of innocence.

Now my son presents me with yet another green apple and as I taste its delicious tartness, he grins. I've never been fully able to accept the humble apple as the cause of so much loss. Apples are the first fruit I remember eating as a child. I loved their slick skin against my teeth, the sharp bite of their flesh on an autumn day in the open air. An apple was my idea of perfection.

Later, apples came to symbolize for me a certain wholeness, the fullness of a woman's own self-development. From flower to fruit, from potential to purpose, a fully realized woman is rich with a trove of imaginative possibility fleshed out in the *gravitas* of her work. She is in possession both of her capacities to nourish the life around her and of her knowledge of her limits. She has learned who she really is. And thus an apple becomes a symbol, if you will, not of woman's weakness and self-betrayal at all, but of her integrity.

I OPEN the jar, and the wonderful, spicy aroma momentarily engulfs me. Like a good old mead, it explodes with a mingling of fruit and smoke, honey and wood, as deep a pleasure to breathe as it will be two months from now to taste on our tongues. Just smelling it calls to mind the tapers and the subdued joy of late Christmas afternoon. After a spare Christmas eve dinner following the evening service, after all the excitement of the packages having been opened, Christmas dinner is a feast of deep and tranquil gratitude.

I smell the apple one last time before I peel, seed, and chop it. Then I drop it into the jar, reseal the whole, and return it to its berth in the cellar.

As I do so, it occurs to me that perhaps a woman's work ever since Eve has been to take up the task of consciousness that was delivered on us with that first loss. Once we've lost the innocence of childhood—the hour on the tandem bike, the heedless play in the neighbor's apple trees—we begin the work of a lifetime. We need to hone our sensitivities and develop our skills in order to leave our gardens and go out into the world to continue the work of *becoming,* the work of sowing and pruning, of grafting and transplanting, that is so necessary to furthering one's journey.

For most women, this is not an easy or straightforward path. I think of the discontinuities and the disappointments in my own life, and the intense labor that has been required to find the right way, again and again.

It is no coincidence that medieval images of the expulsion from Eden often showed Adam carrying a spade and Eve, a hoe or a distaff. The work of cultivation is a work of consciousness. How many of us have not in one form or another had to accept the loss of innocence and expulsion from one imagined paradise after another? The loss of a partner's connection, the loss of an accepted way of being in the world. Often, it is our relationships that plunge us into change. Often too it is our bodies.

I think of Peyton, whose second pregnancy required her to lie in a hospital bed for six weeks to save the life of her unborn child, an experience that led her to return to a long-neglected gift as a painter. I think of Holly and Anne, close friends who have both buried young children. Of Meg, whose painful divorce led her to an unrealized gift for poetry. Or Lori, whose work with the homeless compelled her to join a contemplative order of nuns.

As I wipe the remains of the apple from the counter and prepare to go to work again, I am aware that the goal of all these wasn't to return to innocence but to arrive, transformed, into wisdom.

My own story as I sat on the mountainside gathering fruit seemed to come together, the elements to mingle, then separate, then merge again, my youthful rebellions, my follies and mature accomplishments, all of the betrayals and griefs and unexpected joys, a potpourri that grows ever richer as time works its chemistry. I love the work of gathering, of trying to glean the hidden truths and unexplored directions that all these elements continue to suggest to me, like the hints and undertones of the finished compote.

When I sit down to Christmas dinner, having passed the coffee and served dessert, the complexities in the fruit will be embodied, palpable, almost larger than life for a brief moment on our tongues. In maturity, a woman wants those hints that are hidden in the fruits of her days to be similarly embodied. It is a desire driven by keen inner necessity, this. It is the harvest need to bear witness to the essences of one's life as they are at long last revealed.

On my desk I keep a volume of Rilke's poems. There is one that I am particularly fond of. It reads:

> I love the dark hours of my being
> in which my senses drop into the deep.
> I have found in them, as in old letters,
> my private life, that is already lived through,

and become wide and powerful now, like legends.
Then I know that there is room in me
for a second huge and timeless life.

Powerful, like legends.

My compote has only limited acclaim—my family and a few
close friends. Likewise, my life. But does this make them any less
dear, any less precious, when the hour of celebration arrives?

$\mathcal{L}$oving

WE HAVE LEFT William with Pam, Mitchell, and Perry at their farmhouse in Dorset, Vermont, and continue an hour north to an inn overlooking the banks of Lake Champlain.

The afternoon is pristine. We follow the White River along roads shot through with spectacular autumn foliage, fiery hues the likes of which we haven't seen in years. At last, we arrive for two days and nights of rest, without phones or interruptions. We plan to walk, eat good food, make love, and savor an uninterrupted night's sleep again—simple luxuries that seem so out of reach most days, these days.

From our room, we can look down through trees that line the precipice above the lake and out across its deep blue silences. It has been years, it seems, since we've heard the sound of peace.

As I change out of my travel clothes, I reach to remove my rings, and only now remember that I am lighter these days. I am without them. Last month, they disappeared into the hoarding fist of a three-year-old and have not yet returned. Doubtless, one day I will find a small cluster of rubies and pearls wedged between some sofa pillows or dropped into the sandbox tunnel to China. Until then, I have no regrets. I lay my watch on the lace-covered dresser. I've come to prefer my hands unadorned.

I DON'T REMEMBER when the fever began. It must have been somewhere past Burlington. I suppose that I've needed a weekend like this for a long time and only realize it now when I lie for two hours on the bed under four layers of blankets, fighting swollen glands.

Over the years, I've grown accustomed to these bouts. Some excess always needs to burn off in me. Invariably, I manage to restore myself just when it is nearly too late. But always, it is at a price. For what has seemed an eternity, I lie here flushed, thinking, "I could spend the rest of the weekend in this white and silent room, staring at the ceiling, getting better, body and soul."

*

THIS MORNING when I wake, the fever has cleared. I sense a transformation within. Something has changed in me. Something that has gone unnoticed in the continual press of life's ordinary demands. Perhaps I needed to come away, to be forced to lie still, in order to see it.

I don't leap from bed. Instead, I study the pale-yellow light as it grows brighter against the shades. I feel lighter than I've been in years.

After breakfast, we set out for a long walk. We follow a path that rises between hedgerows on the elevated meadowland. The broad fields have been laid out so that one can see only small, ravishing views, glimpses of the whole horticultural intent, until one arrives at the summit. As we enter one green "room" after another, a glade turning into a small wood, this in turn giving onto a delightful little knoll close by the sounds of a weir, Mark talks about his work, the promise of a certain upcoming political project, the problem with a particularly difficult writer.

I listen, but for the first time, in what has been so much the pattern of exchange woven over many years of marriage, I have no desire to talk in turn about my own. At one point, perhaps baffled by this silence on my part, he jokes that it is refreshing to be away alone with me, without my omnipresent computer and a manuscript that needs revision by Monday. But I don't rise to the bait. I want to simply be here in this gentle place, taking in its beauty.

To meet oneself in this culture, I muse as I look around me, we *need* to do combat in the world of ambition. And perhaps in a more exaggerated way than people in the past have had to do, for we have dispensed with the other traditional rites of passage into adulthood—tests of acumen, courage, and wisdom by which a man or woman was deemed whole and prepared to accept leadership and responsibility. The achieving competitive ego is the only commonly held icon to adulthood that we have by which to judge personhood. Its significance is thereby outsized—almost grotesquely, it sometimes seems to me now. It has produced so many overly busy, self-important, incessantly talking bodies that block out a view of the landscape around them.

To be denied the chance to compete or to be prematurely taken out of the running or to fail to walk up to the mark at all are the most insidious dismemberments from our society that an individual can experience. But to seriously challenge this sanctification of competition on the grounds that it carries with it enormous psychic, moral, and social costs has become inadmissible.

This morning, having burned off my own impedimenta, I invite the inadmissible. It seems to me that women need to take the lead in challenging what we hold to be the satisfactions of our work. So much energy is spent on "show," jockeying for the validation of peers and betters, being seen and rewarded, that it is easy to lose sight of the fact that the greatest pleasure we can know in our work is the total absorption we usually call "flow." To be in flow is to be in the absence of self-consciousness that is the opposite of "show." It is to become invisible, one with the work.

In all of our lives, there comes a point where we know with fair certainty who we are, what we know, and what we have been given by way of talents, gifts, and temperament. The odd new piece of information here or there, the unplanned accomplishment, won't increase or diminish the basic stock one whit; nor will applying our talents in any way "use" them up. This is the point at which we can begin to cultivate the invisibility of flow, which heretofore we've known only in scattered, pleasurable moments, as a continuous "way." And this, I realize as I walk, is the one way that allows us true freedom, the freedom to passionately render ourselves in the moment, without the earlier anxieties and fears of diminishment that bedevil our less developed selves. When we have arrived at this juncture, it seems to me, we are ready to understand love, be it for our work, our children, for the others in our lives.

THE OPEN-AIR ROOMS through which we continue to climb are magnificent in their bold simplicities. Each has something new to reveal, a new bird song, a stone bench, a way of marking open space. Going into nature has often been the catalyst I've needed to return to my own experience of flow.

After three hours, we come out at the summit of the mountain. It is a cascading symphony of colors and tiers that exceed all of our expectations. From its heights, in the cool, clear fall air, we can only look down with astonishment, first that a human eye could have envisioned such a view in the raw, then that it could have worked on so monumental a scale to make it a reality.

One of my finest teachers, the novelist John Hawkes, once described love as "a long, close scrutiny."

I wonder if the master architect of the view I am now witnessing had a similar understanding. Did he trek up the mountain day after day and sit where I am sitting, absorbing its many bends, angles, and natural proclivities, then trek back down and dream awhile, until his design painstakingly emerged?

I imagine that he must have. I imagine that over time this long, close scrutiny underwent a change. After his days and weeks (and probably months) as a professional horticulturist, observing the surfaces, habits, and objective qualities of this mountain as a "thing" to be altered, I imagine that he began to know it differently, as an intimate. I imagine that he began to see through its external appearances to its essence, to a dignity in it that couldn't be changed, but only met, and met not solely nor entirely on the basis of his professional skills, but by the inner man who had done the deep and true seeing. Standing at the heights taking in the harmonies of intent and finished execution before us, I can feel this transparency of motive in the quality of the whole. He bent to the life before him.

MANY YEARS AGO, I encountered my first experience of this kind of love in the mother of my childhood friend Molly. By the time I met her, Mrs. Boylan was an older woman with a beautiful mane of white hair that she pinned up each morning into a wispy French twist.

Though the thought didn't occur to me when I was ten, I am now certain that Mrs. B. must have experienced a rich erotic life before she settled into the stately grace that I knew in her. The sort of love that begins in a startling, insatiable possessiveness and ends by dipping its hem into the holy because it is led there, the sort of love in which the entanglements of the body are just the soul's way of keeping itself attached to the earth. I am certain because I am old enough to have experienced the same and to recognize the hold of her bearing, the confidence and depth of her gaze.

She bore six children, and in between their cat's cradle of continual demands, I heard an unmistakable lilt in her voice whenever she exchanged words with her husband. Once, I saw him take her in his arms and carry her up the stairs.

She kept a household that was devoted in every nuance to the spirit of creativity. The grand piano was perpetually littered with musical scores and the notation pages of her offsprings' compositions. Books in several languages lay open on the sofas and floor, for her husband's favorite relaxation was to read Homer in the original Greek. Paintings leaned on the stairs leading to the children's bedrooms. Flowers bloomed in vases and towering bushes around the house.

The children's time in Mrs. B's house was one continuous improvisation. Early morning found us in the kitchen where a loaf of fresh baked bread would be consumed as cinnamon toast, then up to the bedrooms where we'd commandeer the velvet curtains, the satin coverlet, a handful of old jewelry, for our Shakespeare skits; then out to the loft above the garage where we held our secret meetings.

Only in the subtlest but most penetrating way was Mrs. B. a presence in her own home. I was, and remain, certain that it was she who set the muses in motion each day. She who enchanted or ignited the geniuses in her husband and children. She who, having sent them on their ways, retreated to her own room for reading, letter writing, and the general fostering of life around her.

Surely it was she who saw to it that food was on the table at night and the laundry in the proper rooms. Yet I never witnessed a mundane act performed at her hands. Surely she saw to her children's manners and deportment, but I never heard her utter a word of reproof. What order and harmony prevailed under her rule emerged from a deeper place, a place of faith in the goodness of minds engaged, in laughter, and in the rightness of her role in encouraging and maintaining the atmosphere of her home.

Often I watched her, walking among her apple trees reading Emily Dickinson or refinishing an old cupboard. At a child's subconscious level, I was sure that she was being fed by these activities, for I never saw her flustered, nor anything but at deep peace. She was ever accessible yet sweetly detached. Every afternoon, she set off with the family's large sheep dog for a three-mile walk.

As feminists we renounced this kind of loving. But it seems to me now that we did so only because we failed to see it as the template of all worthy love and all good work that await us at the turning point, when we are finally able to relate to life as one transparency to another, when we are able to act from the essence.

Mrs. B., whom I knew late in her life when her chief comfort was Emily Dickinson in the garden, had traveled into and through the place of possessive love and had learned its secrets. Unfettered self-giving isn't possible without full possession. We cannot possibly give of ourselves without first having held ourselves and been held dear, whether as achieving egos or as lovers. But if in the end, our lives are to be more than bright vectors of self-gratification, we must come to see ourselves as part of a larger story, one whose legacy has sustained us and will outlast us.

In another generation, Mrs. Boylan would perhaps have become an artist. Instead, she planted the seeds from which her daughters flowered, and in the art of her loving gave them the model of love that has served as the model for their work. One became a writer, one a painter, one a musician. Where peers have produced timidly, desirous of critical acclaim, her daughters have

moved well beyond, given a complete rendering, in works of deep
generosity and transparency, of genuine quality and originality.

WE START DOWN the hill, retracing our steps, to get back to the
inn and a fire before dinner. Soon, I think, the wind will sing its
clearest notes through my denuded arbor back home. In my body
at midlife, I begin to feel too the preparations for a greater transparency, greater humility and inwardness. I need more sleep, toler-
ate wine badly, toss at night if I've had too late an evening. Caffeine
gives me headaches. I find myself turning to nuts and vegetables
again, much as I did when I was pregnant. I like the feel of a certain
hunger in my belly, postpone a meal, sidle into a fast.

In this culture, it is hard to attune ourselves to these signals of the
flesh. We fear them. They spell diminishment—of stamina, independence, mental acuity. But perhaps there is another way to look
at it. Perhaps the body and mind are saying that they want no
impediments now to a full rendering of the self.

Once a woman has passed through the many rooms of love—
erotic love, maternal love, the love of conformist ambition—she
arrives at a clear place where it is possible to act from a new, more
transparent self. Work no longer entails the superhuman effort to
possess or to master, but instead the desire to surrender. It is a spiritual act, a burning through from the place within, the place of endless opening out, endless flowering, that is only provisionally held
in our flesh and bones. A higher force seems to have entered into
us, working in and through us, and passing out again.

Our needs become significantly reduced without our being fully
aware of it. What fulfills us *is* less material. We still enjoy good food
and wine, but we love as much the kneading, the cutting, the
smells of baking, the vision of the meal before the work of preparation begins. Likewise, we're less anxious to acquire. We're grateful

to pick and choose, to circulate through objects, favorite gifts that over time and use have accrued their value. The body says to clear itself to feast on rarer fare, to rid ourselves of ornament and pearls, pull back to the treasures within.

In his Preface to *Paradise Lost*, C. S. Lewis once wrote this about the creation of a great poem: "The attempt to be oneself often brings out only the more conscious and superficial parts of a man's mind; working to produce a given kind of poem which will present a given theme as justly, delightfully, and lucidly as possible, he is more likely to bring out all that was really in him, and much of which he himself had no suspicion."

We have reached the inn—and just in time, for the wind is picking up. Tea is being served, but I opt for a quiet perch by the fire. If I can respect the voice of winter pressing me on, I will be more open to the greater transparency, the greater way of loving, that I want to open up in me.

I turn to an exhibition catalog of Corot's works that sits on the side table. Midway through there is a photograph that draws and keeps my attention, long after the tea has been cleared and the fire tamped down. It is of Corot as an old man. He is alone in the woods with his few tools, seated somewhat awkwardly on a camp stool, just looking.

WE PULLED INTO the farmhouse drive just as the boys were crouching in a tepee made of cornstalks from Pam's garden. I feel an amazing, religious sense of peace. A sureness and gratitude that has been with me since I awakened this morning and simply accepted who I am and loved myself—with no anxiety, no need to rush, to prove myself, no regrets, and no need to retreat to seek a center that I've somehow let slip.

I want to simply lean against a tree and watch the children chase

Mitchell, their sticks as swords, then lie face up to the sky as he blows balloons and sends them scampering after them. We've brought apples and cookies, and soon all of us are sitting on the porch, waving away flies and holding the little ones on our knees.

As we are driving home in the dark, the rain begins. From the backseat, I hear a small voice.

"I'm tired, Mommy. Can *you* make a little yawn for me, Mommy?"

Of this, the pearls of my days are made.

$\mathcal{D}$ying

I AM WORKING in my office one afternoon when the phone rings. It is Linda's husband.

"I'm calling to tell you," says the strangely formal voice, "because she can't bear to. Linda was treated for malignant breast cancer two weeks ago."

My senses go into overdrive. I am registering every detail of this moment as if it were my last, and it seems that there aren't enough details. Or that I can't get enough of them from this conversation for it to make any sense.

I hear: a 1.5-centimeter cyst. Missed during a regular mammogram last October. Missed again by the mammogram she requested after she discovered it in the shower. A sonogram and a local biopsy confirmed the truth.

The node scan, negative. The treatment protocol: a summer of chemotherapy, followed by a long autumn of radiation.

"The doctors are optimistic. Her survival rate is ninety-five percent."

I stare out the window on a brilliant day in springtime. The illusions of endless possibility have just fallen away. I come face to face with what I've always known that I must one day. There are no exceptions. Mortality is as intimate as my hand holding the receiver. We are all living on borrowed time.

"Call her," says S.

I DO. I learn that I was just blocks from her apartment, doing a reading, while she sat in her living room with her awful knowledge, alone. I learn that she proceeded to throw a book party just hours after learning the news, entertaining hundreds of her husband's well-wishers. Only when it was all over was she able to make room for *her* story, a postscript to the celebration of life that she'd managed once again to pull off.

THE MONTHS COMPLETE their purgatory. We journey to the country house to celebrate the end of treatments, bringing a fig tart for S., flowers for Linda, and lots of distractions for our now quite mobile youngster. Everything is as it always has been, the quiet rhythms, the comings and goings of the large extended clan.

S. cooks a pheasant he caught last spring, and the next day, we hike. L. and S. practicing for another much-anticipated Montana trek in July.

But L. is very tired—a holdover from the chemo, she assures us. She promises to be in better spirits when we see her in six weeks in South Carolina.

But Linda doesn't come to South Carolina. The day before we depart she calls complaining of a flu bug she can't shake.

The night of our return, I come into my office to check my messages. There is a call from Avice, a mutual friend. Linda's cancer has metastasized crazily, from breast to femur, hips, spine, and head. She was admitted to New York University Medical Center the day after we spoke, on the verge of kidney failure.

I suddenly remember the night, many years ago, when we walked home through the wet, blowing leaves from a Muddy Waters concert.

I remember our afternoons at Quabbin.

At Galilee, with its birds and clam cakes and its little fishing shacks. The memories overwhelm me.

I'd always imagined us growing old together.

AN ARMY OF WOMEN descends on Linda's apartment, grieving, gentle, caring, and full of unexpressed prayers. We are available in waves—to help her to the bathroom, prepare her tea, hold her hand and talk, listen, or simply to be silent.

There are so many of us that schedules have to be drawn up and dates assigned. And it seems as though we women have nothing else to do and never did than to nurse.

We are passing Linda along, a powerful chain of hands, into hands we cannot see but feel with each gesture of care and love that we make.

The men in the picture (and there *are* men: a husband, a brother) do not give days. They are too busy, still carrying on with the world. Grieving, too. Occasionally seeing to logistics.

But we women seem to come by this so naturally, I'm not sure whether to be saddened or proud. The sister of mercy in us all is a gift as ancient as Mary and Martha. It is a bearing on the culture at its most rudimentary and essential. Without our hands, it is evident to me today, life would simply not exist. Even with so many other demands on our time, the chosen demands of our intellects and talents, we readily throw ourselves into a work that informs us, our marrow, from nameless generations. We recognize in ourselves the *need* to do this work. To pretend otherwise is to deny our Selves.

Bright pink and red tulips stand everywhere in tall vases. We see to them. Wrens and finches still gambol outside the living-room windows by well-stocked feeders; the oxalis stands moist and serene in its dish on pebbles. And all around us, the familiar baskets of books, newspapers, *New Yorkers*, and catalogs are maintained in this den devoted to the printed word.

In the midst of all this, it is sobering and shocking to find my dear Linda so whittled away. She is gray, translucent. Her skin strangely perfect in suffering. She rests against her walker to laboriously pull up a sock, tries to laugh it off, but winces instead at the rocketing pain in her left hip. Her head is bald.

Jenny arrives, and while the physical therapist teaches Linda to manage stairs around her pain, we set out in search of lamb, strawberries, artichokes, and good bread, the fixings for a feast, as if no one is dying, in the memory and the manner of all the days of innocence and gladness past.

We cook and chop vegetables and talk and cry and hope together. Linda joins us at the table, heroically keeping up her end of things as we grieve silently to ourselves and drink cups of sweet tea and two bottles of red wine.

When it is over, Jenny and I step out into the damp night and walk around several blocks to settle our souls for the night.

How does one settle one's soul in the face of such loss, such untimeliness? We look into the Barneys window; we laugh a little. Almost convincing ourselves that all is as it always has been.

We are going to need kindness, patience, tolerance, and grace to get us through this. We're going to need precious hours well spent:

talking of books, of poetry, of eating well, and uncorking good wine, feeding our souls on the too quickly passing feast.

"We're going to need one another," says Jenny.

And we pass under the awning, out of the night, and into the lit vestibule once more.

The next day, I have the afternoon shift, as Jenny is going out. Linda is feverish with talk. Desperate to impart her incredulity, her pain, her infinite and abject sense of failure. She does not want to die childless. She doesn't want to die without having realized her dream of becoming a poet.

I cast about in my mind for what might buoy her through this suffering—works, parables, poems, even paintings. I finally decide to tell her her own story.

It was she who, though she never published a work of her own, showed us how the life of a poet ought to be lived. It was she who'd had the courage to move to New York to write. She who read ceaselessly and deeply; who shared poems and later, her love of birds and opera; she who never lost faith in her friends through all of their periods of darkness and confusion.

Linda gave us the courage to be artists, thinkers, to be strong in what set us apart. We never left Linda's presence without being changed by her vision of us. Linda was the force behind so many of our efforts, the enthusiast when our confidence flagged, the support during the dim times. Over and over again, she created the medium in which we found our voices, our pitch, our work. She was a teacher without a classroom; a guide whose intuitive shrewdness and sense of beauty drew us to her, to be inspired, affirmed, refreshed. She has been an instinctively wise woman too passionately engaged until now to ever stop and realize how rare her gift really is.

She has gone very quiet. I search my heart. How can I help her heal in the only way that matters now? What are the steps to true healing, the initiation into that deepest meaning of "going home," that we might enter together, as we once entered into poems and into silence, this time with me on the threshold and her proceeding on, alone.

I lie down on the bed and take her hand, our heads close on the pillow. There is nothing more to say, except the only thing.

I love you.

I love you too.

TWO DAYS OF readjustment to being home, the usual busyness. Then, last night before dinner, I went upstairs and pulled the comforter tight around me on the bed. I don't often have the luxury to fall into my feelings, but I did so now.

Great gulfs of blackness have been threatening since I returned, rising into tidal waves only when I have the strength to acknowledge them. At the most important strata, I've been paralyzed. Competent, but at the level where thought and creativity count, inert. A stone. Unable to concentrate on work or to remember much. In the maw of depression. Undertow.

On the bed, I sank. I looked out at the hillside of stripped trees and gray sky and realized that it has been nearly two years since I saw my father for the last time. The sky had looked just like this one.

So all the deaths reiterate themselves.

My mother, like a shadow, passive with depression. With effort, we lifted our arms and voices, moved in the old rhythms, did the old things. Bill and Libby came around with the baby and we took the boys to a playground on the raw Saturday—only to have flashbacks to Tim's funeral, on the same kind of day.

Geographies take on haunted spots, ghosts, energy centers—and out there my family, living in the midst of them, burdened, almost suffocated, by them.

It is this snuffing out, all of these shadows and burials, that I've carried back here.

LINDA HAS BEEN in the hospital since Friday. Dementia. Huge calcium outputs. Calls from Jenny, Avice, Darlyn.

She appeared to be slipping into a coma, was briefly sent home, alert, then ordered readmitted. To all outsiders' bafflement, the doctors have decided to begin Taxol treatment immediately, after saying they'd keep her on Tamoxifin through June. The closer I look at it, the angrier I get. Aren't they just prolonging her suffering? What, except protecting themselves in the face of an obvious medical disaster, are they trying to accomplish?

Life, precious gift.

LAST NIGHT, I dreamed about Linda. A resurrection dream. It involved both of us, her place in my soul, my understanding of her life. After years of our marriages to other people, we rediscovered our "first" loves and were returning to them, to marry them. I found Linda in the upper reaches of an old-world New York club. It was a warm, wooded place, full of the atmosphere of good books and brandy, white linens, and heavy silver. She had just returned from house hunting in Princeton.

In the dream, I was surprised briefly and felt a twinge of loss. Princeton seemed so far away. Further, her recovered life would involve much travel. She wanted to go to the sacred sites around the world and study at each of them.

I felt selfishly bereft until I realized that I wasn't losing Linda but was in fact gaining the deep poetic spirit of the artist I'd first known so many years earlier, when we were students and young writers. The woman of deep refinement and subtle taste and restrained beauty had returned. She looked radiantly herself, as I haven't seen her in months.

*

AT 4 A.M. Sunday morning, I woke, unable to sleep. I went down to the living room and opened the *Book of Common Prayer*, something I have never done before. I read the prayer for Compline.

"Keep watch, dear Lord, with those who work, or watch, or weep this night, and give your angels charge over those who sleep. Tend the sick, Lord Christ; give rest to the weary, bless the dying, soothe the suffering, pity the afflicted, shield the joyous; and all for your love's sake. Amen."

TWENTY-THREE HOURS LATER, exactly, at 3 a.m. on Monday morning, my friend breathed her last.

> East River and the pale row houses—
> Ash and bone and chalk—
> A morning of fog lights and empty playing fields.
> Stone has a solace that her dying face can't assume
> Can't, though it incandesces with courage, assure.
> The empty sockets of old warehouses
> The usual bad coffee
> I am whispering goodbyes
> On the backside of everything:
> City, daylight, a woman's face.
> The landscape out there
> Is one long wailing wall.

I remember the tall vases
Proud in their vigilance
Over her bed
Suspending for one yesterday
Our eternal twilight.

*

FRIENDS ARRIVE in the country after weeks in various cities, settling in among the horses and dogs and relations. We are weighted down with memories, gathering one last time with our smoked mozzarella, cherry tomatoes, good wines. Into a place where the doors have no locks, the bounty no doors. All weekend, friends drop by for cappuccino, turning the stalks of the daffodils Linda would have placed in pitchers of water in the middle of the kitchen table, gossiping while she kneaded dough or sliced apples. If she were still here, at dawn, she might have driven once again along rutted roads through rain to fetch eggs from the caretaker's chicken coop, familiar hounds coming out to bay, a family of farmers from down the road passing, their women's boots slapped with mud beneath their skirts.

All was benign back then. All was innocence.

We gather to remember what she was always teaching us, that love never dies.

Heart-bird

Turnstone, heart-bird, we distinguish
ourselves by our habits. You find
your food beneath a stone. I hear,
when I come to the shore, not
the wind or the sea but the thunder
of stones turning over and over.

Come out of the marsh. Come down to the beach, this clutter of
stones. Among them is my
own — irregular rough, dun-colored.
You cannot know which one it is.

One day you will turn it over, bend
down, fold your chestnut
wings across your black breast,
and see what I have left.

LINDA CORRENTE, 1953–1999

Rebirth

ANOTHER MONTH HAS come and gone.

Yesterday, I went to see Mrs. W., we both knew, for the last time. Neither of us is foolish enough to suppose that all of the questions have been answered, all the loose threads sewn up. But it wasn't the time to open new chapters. Instead, she suggested that I free-associate to see whether any final business wanted to come up after three years of hard inner work.

I closed my eyes and found myself returning to the painful emotions surrounding the book project that I let go, unfinished. Even now! I thought. It was as if all this time it's been frozen in ice, a battered image grown more unreal, more grotesque, more inaccessible—a symbol of a failure despite the fact that it launched me on the most important journey of my life.

As I talked and recollected, something amazing happened.

All of the self-lacerating criticism, the judgments and avoidance, the rationalizations and the coping strategies I'd used to distance myself from the pain at the time—all evaporated. In their place, the human beings at the center of the story reappeared, as clear and beautiful as an autumn day: the poor children and their mothers, the teachers and social workers, all of them working so hard to make a better life for one another.

I felt such love for them, I was astonished. I had always loved them, I realized. I realized too that my biggest failure had been allowing my pride and anger to obscure this fact from me. I felt a crushing sadness at the layers of resistance I'd put between myself and them, levels of theorizing, interpretation, words, thoughts, elegant arguments—all out of a fear that there was nothing, no foundation, no story, underneath. As if their lives, alone, weren't enough.

Mrs. W., who has *never once* interrupted me, did so now.

"You have just described your own life," she said quietly.

I stopped, stunned. She was right. This was how I *had* lived my life, buried beneath layers of intellectualization, caught in a world of ideas that I'd allowed to pass for a real life. I saw something else. I saw that I no longer need the layering, the ruses, the analysis and intellectualization, because I am no longer afraid of love. This is what the journey has been all about. I have healed.

I RETURNED HOME and went into the garden and worked there for a long while, William digging holes nearby. The season of silence is about to come around again. The cherry tomatoes are red and fat on their vines; the basil has already bolted. To be given another chance; to recover, or rediscover, the meaning of one's life—what greater gift can a woman receive at midlife?

I feel as if I can begin to make whole, to make holy. To live a Sabbath life.

After a simple meal of brown rice and squash, broccoli rabe, and apples, I fell into a sound sleep.

I dreamed that I was back in Mrs. W.'s office, only this time she was just a symbolic presence. More real and mesmerizing by far were her collections of primitive pots: ceremonial flasks and urns, some carved from very dark woods, others of woods that have calcified into stone. There were ebonies inlaid with ivory, mother-of-pearl, worn to a lustrous polish by centuries of touch.

Old forms. Ancient containers. Primitive, fundamental, age affirmed, and beautiful. Hadn't I been looking for a new container for my life?

I woke and made a cup of tea. I watched a pale sunrise, thinking about the virgin place in each of us and about the creator who makes us new with the most basic materials available. With earth, water, the body, and fire. With time.

Shortly after breakfast, Mr. Fertado arrived. His vast rattling landscaper's truck hardly made it down the lane with its armature of loud, motorized saws, mowers, and blowers. He came somewhat unwillingly, because today he must work alone and because he is accustomed to grander places than mine.

I've asked him to edge the lawn, prune the bushes in front, and cut off the deadwood on the crabs in back. I've given him a full day's work and he goes at it doggedly, yanking, hauling, filling the back of his pickup with refuse on its way to becoming mulch. He is astonishingly strong and blunt in his dealings with the plants. Dogged and without, I can't help feeling, the requisite love.

As a result, though I hadn't intended to, I soon find myself in the garden as well, prowling protectively. The grape leaves list against the vines, rusted and chapped. The husks of the roses rattle and nod. The wind, if not the force of Fertado, will blow them free before long. But are they not in their own way without beauty? The hostas alongside the garden house will shrink to underground corms, but in so doing they'll expose the river stones that I have lovingly gathered over a thousand visits to the shore, to Canada, Menemsha, and elsewhere.

All of these forms, if they are healthy, will return in good time. Even the clothespin that I find lying in the grass by the chokecherry will resurrect its purposes next July. Even a gourd, fallen from the compost pile.

Trimmed, pruned, quiescent, the absence of the riotous things will reveal the garden's underlying design. In the chill winds of November, I will remember why I set the trellis ever so slightly turned to the west. I will recall the rose-bearing barrel's sculptural purpose atop the shorn ash stump. Pared, more linear and spare, the garden can speak the language of essences. I'll see more clearly what ought to stay, what ought to be moved, what replaced, before the riot of fertility resumes.

A woman begins her life in innocence, as dream, as gift. It evolves its timbre to sustain her. And for a long time afterward, we call this flourishing. But inevitably, much of what we do becomes routine rather than creative. It grows knotted, gnarled, and we may not at first see that there *is* deadwood no longer producing good fruit.

We may not even see that our beloved garden has become something we hadn't intended, full of weeds, overgrown, or pollinated in ways we couldn't have predicted.

Then, one day, we spy a flash of something new, white, and young among the grasses, or brown and fungal among the dying leaves. And it evokes in us a desire so pure that try as we might to silence our hearts, we are led to it.

We kneel, look, and see. It is the symbol of our lost oneness, obscured like everything else by the accretions of habit and age. In the rose, the green of the immature grape, the hieroglyphs of birds on the beach, in the newborn, the poem, in any one of a million humble, everyday things, we see the possibility of the gift restored, the place we've lost track of, the place of unending creativity.

To begin again is to honor the fact of impermanence. It is to acknowledge and accept death, alongside regeneration and rebirth. This is the place in us where creativity and responsibility meet, where women can begin to learn what it means for us to live Sabbath lives.

THIS IS NOT for the tenderhearted. It is tough, radical, hard. Mr. Fertado has finished tearing knotted vines and wisteria from out of the picket fence and is climbing onto the roof of the garden house, clippers in hand, to behead the exuberant crabs. A bough comes off clean to the base of the trunk. Stalks the breadth of his thick man's arm fall and break against the hard earth. Tears spring to my eyes. I know that the trees will be healthier, come spring, but this doesn't offset the pain.

I bring the clothespin and the gourd indoors with me and place them on the table next to the plate of asparagus I've set out to steam for dinner.

The gourd was once a butternut squash. It is mottled and cracked now as the finest raku pot. I think about the arc of its life, from seed to flower to fruit, picked clean by passing field mice then left to age, a hollow shell, an object so completely and irreversibly transformed as to be unrecognizable to the next generation of young buds.

Did the flower "know" when to send out its fruit? Or the fruit when to render its seed and surrender to the earth?

Sitting beside the asparagus on my kitchen table, it becomes an emblem of transformation, of the evolving nature of a woman's integrity across the span of a life, of the creative possibilities that come with a certain emptiness, a lack of obvious purpose.

I have planted and cultivated the garden of midlife. Now it is time to open myself to stories and the echoes of stories beyond my own, to step out again onto the soil of the world, to share its tables, break its breads, and eat its fruits, in ways that I have yet to learn.

I admire the way the purples of the fresh asparagus and the golds of the gourd dance and rhyme off one another. And I know that within me, seasoned and flawed as I may have become, a new thing wants to bloom.